The Successful Supervisor

THE
SUCCESSFUL
SUPERVISOR

In Government and Business

Third Edition

by William R. Van Dersal

1817

HARPER & ROW, PUBLISHERS

NEW YORK, HAGERSTOWN,

SAN FRANCISCO, LONDON

Library of Congress Cataloging in Publication Data

Van Dersal, William Richard, 1907–

   The successful supervisor in government and business.

   Bibliography: p.

   1. Supervision of employees. I. Title.

HF5549.V29 1974   658.3′02   73–4134

ISBN 0–06–014487–4

To my wife, Helen

Contents

Preface   *vii*

1   *Some Preliminary Ideas*   1

2   *Basic Principles of Supervision*   10

3   *Supervisor's Expectations*   23

4   *Some Techniques in Supervising*   33

5   *Participation*   46

6   *Something About Motivation*   62

7   *New Insights into Human Behavior*   82

8   *Training*   91

9   *Communications*   112

10   *About Organizations*   132

11   *Some Management Activities*   150

12   *Solving Problem Cases*   170

13   *Books and Journals*   192

Index   199

Preface

This book was written for practicing supervisors, whether in government, business, industry, or elsewhere, and whether in high positions or low. Supervision has to do with influencing human action in organizations doing work. The policies and procedures of these organizations may differ widely and so may their objectives, but scarcely the fundamental nature of their supervisory problems.

There are no panaceas in this book, and its writer makes no claim to being an expert. What I have written here summarizes what I have learned over many years by observing, analyzing, and studying both successful and unsuccessful supervisors.

One of the things that helped me a great deal in this endeavor was a project undertaken in 1945 by T. Roy Reid, at that time director of personnel for the United States Department of Agriculture. He wrote a personal letter to each of some five hundred supervisors who were named as the best in that large department by their various bureau chiefs. He asked the supervisors to write him a letter explaining what they thought was most important in supervising people, and describing something of the methods and techniques used in their work.

The replies, from all parts of the country, made a stack about three feet high. This I remember well because I had the opportunity of studying these letters for months. Some were brief. Some were many pages in length, but all were sincere and packed with ideas. Gradually, I came to distinguish those key ideas which, if they appeared in one letter, were likely to appear in most or all of the others. These ideas, some seven in number, and common to the five hundred supervisors, are expressed in Chapter 2 as general principles.

Over the past twenty-eight years I have discussed these ideas, or principles, as well as many other aspects of supervision, with thousands of supervisors—in the federal government, in state governments, in foreign governments, in businesses, and in industry. I have subjected the principles to critical discussion in dozens of formal management training courses, as well as in my classes in supervision at the Graduate School of the United States Department of Agriculture and at Colorado State University, Columbia University, North Carolina State University, and a number of others. Besides this, they have been reproduced and used in a large number of agencies of the federal government and in agencies of many foreign governments. All told, they have undergone a certain amount of modification, although the concepts they express have stood up remarkably well. In a very real sense, these ideas have been validated by tens of thousands of years of supervisory experience. This extensive testing should, I believe, generate reasonable confidence in their substance.

In addition to this experience, I have also been combing the literature for ideas and techniques of possible value to practicing supervisors. Whatever I have found that seemed of possible use I have promptly put to the test either in management and supervisory courses or classes, or in my own organization, or in both. It became clear to me long ago that there was a serious gap between academic theory and the everyday practice of supervision.[1] I found great difficulty in trying to bridge that gap. I suggest it as one reason why supervisors generally do not seem to be avid readers of the professional books in their field.

It has often seemed to me that the science of human relations—if, indeed, it may be called a science—is one of the

1. Others have expressed this idea. For example, see Lyndall F. Urwick, "Management and Human Relations," in *Leadership and Organization*, by R. Tannenbaum, I. R. Wechsler, and F. Massarik (New York: McGraw-Hill Book Co., 1961), pp. 416–428; and "Notes on a General Theory of Administration," *Administrative Science Quarterly*, June 1956, pp. 1–29.

poorest and most confused of them all. In fact, if there is any one thing that seems clear about us, it is that we do not yet seem to know how to get along with each other very well —at work, at home, in private life, in public life, in our own country, or as between nations. Since most adult Americans work, and since nearly all of them are supervised in their work, or supervise others, perhaps attempting to improve the quality of supervision could have an important effect on human relations in general. However, I have had no such project in mind. If I can help supervisors at least to approach their supervisory tasks and problems on a common-sense, intelligent basis, I shall have succeeded in achieving the goal I had in mind when I collected the material for and wrote this book.

In the twelve years since the first edition of this book, I have enjoyed a multitude of opportunities to talk and work and correspond with practicing supervisors. They number in the thousands, and they have come from various types of organizations, in both this country and a large number of other countries. In the meantime, a flood of new books and a monthly deluge of magazines and journal articles have offered new information, some of it of considerable value. Since this book has had a rather wide use as a text or reference in courses at universities and other institutions, I felt it necessary to bring it up to date.

The fact is that supervisors bear a heavy responsibility that too few of them seem to realize. The way a supervisor works with his people can, and frequently does, affect significantly his people's careers, and indeed their lives. An approach based on prejudice, a decision based in ignorance, a careless remark based on indifference, can easily lead to injustice and, in certain settings, to disaster. As many scientists in the fields of sociology, psychology, and associated areas have pointed out, we have a long way to go before we have enough facts on which to base our understanding of each other. One day perhaps, supervisors will possess the sure knowledge enabling them to deal with their people in a fully enlightened way. In the meantime, supervisors everywhere owe it to their people, no less than to themselves, to keep informed of the best and most factual information available to help them deal reasonably with their associates.

My studies of supervision and management and my experience with supervisors have led me to conclude that there is little significant difference between supervision in government agencies, businesses, industries, and other organizations.[2] This appears to be true both in the United States and in at least fifty other countries with whose representatives I have had opportunities to work. Problems with human beings at work are basically similar no matter where they occur. In the area of human relations, supervisors of whatever "level," or status, or salary, or title, or national origin, or skin color, or sex, seem to be faced with common problems. In all my hundreds of groups, with any mixture of supervisors, I have never experienced a situation in which the supervisors had difficulty understanding each other's problems. Variations in human nature seem to be as great between any two individual supervisors as between groups of supervisors from different kinds of organizations, "levels," or countries.

The nature of human beings is such that human uniqueness and similarity are distributed worldwide. It is not different because of culture, institutions, or religion. Human nature is much more fundamental in character than any of these distinctions. I suggest that it is about time we learned and took seriously what the great religious leaders, philosophers, educators, and thinkers have been telling us for centuries upon centuries. How shall we, indeed, deal with our fellow man?

2. Harvey Sherman has also expressed this idea in his book *It All Depends,* reviewed briefly on page 196.

The Successful Supervisor

1   *Some Preliminary Ideas*

There are few jobs more difficult but at the same time more interesting than that of supervising people. This takes more skill, more common sense, more imagination, more good humor, and certainly as much intelligence as any other kind of work. And it can frequently hold more grief, more trouble, and more difficulties than other kinds of work, particularly for the man or woman who has not learned the art of working with other people.

Most people who work were employed in the first place not because they could supervise, but because they had some other skill or knowledge needed to perform a job. People enter the government service as they enter business or industry, first of all because they are willing to work—a qualification of basic importance (though we sometimes take it for granted). They may be unskilled, in which case their willingness to work is possibly all they have to offer. They may be skilled, in which case they come to their jobs as carpenters, typists, stenographers, mechanics, laboratory technicians, or some other kind of skilled worker. Many others come to their jobs well trained in accounting, engineering, biology, forestry, law, chemistry, physics, or in other scientific or professional fields, and most of these go through four or more years of college or university training. Few, even of these, are employed originally as supervisors.

Eventually, some of these people who do a good job—skilled, unskilled, or professional—are put in charge of a group of other people and designated as supervisors.

This is a major change. The new supervisor cannot rely on the skill or knowledge of his former work to help him solve the many new problems facing him. No matter how skilled a mechanic he was, no matter how good an accountant, no matter how much law or science he might know, he is not therefore automatically able to supervise people. He encounters difficult and stubborn problems in human relations, communications, and management. These do not yield to manual dexterity or to the principles of the sciences or professions in which he might have been trained. He must fall back on what he knows from general experience in order to solve problems that may often prove to be of great complexity and difficulty. This, in a thousand variations, is what has happened to supervisors almost everywhere.

When a new supervisor begins to realize his own deficiencies—and there are some who never do, of course—he may do one of several things. He may request a transfer to his old work and thank his stars that he is back among familiar things. Or he may rock along as best he can on what little he knows or thinks he knows. Or, he may systematically go about the task of equipping himself to operate as skillfully as he is able in the new field of supervision.

In this illustration—endlessly repeated in agencies and organizations of every description—it is clear that a man cannot divorce himself entirely from the work situation out of which he was promoted. Nor should he try. Actually, a supervisor usually continues to work in much the same environment as before. He continues to work with people who are doing the same kind of work that he was doing before. What he does as a supervisor, however, is now different from what he used to do as one of the workers. The contribution he is now expected to make to the work of the organization requires knowledge and ability that he exercised only to a limited degree, if at all, in his former job.

In fact, a person who has become a supervisor has entered what has been recognized for some time as a professional field of its own. In this field there exists a large body of knowledge that a supervisor must know and understand. Many competent people have written about the subject matter involved. There is, indeed, an enormous library of material, which is growing rapidly as new developments continue.

It is true that those with scientific training may consider supervision and management to be less scientific in character than chemistry, or physics, or the other exact sciences. And they would be right. It is a field in which the results are much more difficult to predict. But this need not detract from the progress already made, nor does it invalidate the painfully learned lessons of experience. It would, indeed, be well if more scientists were in this field, for they might bring to it the kind of thinking and the method of approach familiar in their own disciplines.

At any rate, a new supervisor who realizes his need for development in the professional field of supervision can help himself in a number of ways. As he goes about this, let him realize that he is not alone! By far the majority of supervisors have had to do it, and the chances are reasonably good that he can do it, too. Here are some of the ways:

1. Many books have been written about supervision, human relations, executive development, management, administration, and related subjects. Any supervisor ought to know the best books in his field, and it would be well for him to get together at least a small personal library of his own. If he can learn to read these books critically, testing what they say against experience, he can get much of value from them. Chapter 13 tells about some of these books and indicates which may be helpful in this endeavor.

2. A number of professional journals and magazines contain new ideas and new developments in the field of supervision and management. Some of these are listed in the last chapter. Most of these journals can be borrowed from a library, and a supervisor can get the one or two he comes to value most by subscribing to them. This usually means joining a professional society, and this, too, is a useful thing to do. At the periodic meetings of such societies a supervisor can meet other people engaged in the same kind of work. He can exchange ideas and techniques with them, and he can hope to get new points of view about his tougher problems.

3. There is always, of course, the possibility of enrolling in courses offered by colleges and universities in one phase or another of supervisory work. There are night courses, short courses, special workshops or conferences, and home study courses. They, like books, can help a supervisor learn, although they cannot solve his problems for him.

4. The supervisor really trying to improve himself can use another way. He can review and analyze, as objectively as he is able, the way in which he himself is working and getting results. Many people find this procedure difficult to follow. It comes more easily with experience, possibly because a more mature mind can acknowledge mistakes more readily. Self-analysis is never easy, because most of us habitually try to excuse or rationalize what we have done. Rather than admit even to himself that he was in error, a new supervisor is likely to use his self-appraisal primarily to convince himself that he was basically right in whatever he did. Of course, the question is not whether he was right or wrong, but whether he was successful in getting some one or all of his people to perform correctly and productively.

At any rate, the critical and thoughtful review of his own work by a supervisor can guide him toward better ways of operating. If he can be as critical of himself as he can of other people, if he can clearly imagine himself in the position of others, then what he may conclude can often prove of great value in future work. Sometimes one's wife or husband can help with this appraisal, sometimes a close friend (*not* in the supervisor's unit), sometimes another supervisor. But the need for evaluation of one's own performance is clear. The results are far superior to experience alone; they are evaluated experience.

Kinds of Supervision and Supervisors

Many years ago I accidentally stumbled on a teaching device in a group where our discussions about supervision were having heavy going. Too many of the people in the class seemed to have a deep-seated resentment about supervisors as they had known them. In some desperation I stopped the discussion and suggested we make a list of examples of poor supervisory practice. The items flooded forth so fast it was scarcely possible to get them written on the blackboard. When I began to challenge an occasional idea, interesting and useful discussions resulted.

The aftermath was curious. After the discussion, in which feelings sometimes ran high, the group temper changed. As if eager to compensate for their expressed resentment, the participants became constructive. They worked hard at explaining and discussing what they thought good supervision ought to be. Since then, I have begun many conferences or classes on supervision with the same device. It is easy to get people to say what they *do not* like about supervision. They let off a good bit of steam; they seem to like to do it; and unfortunately nearly everyone seems to have plenty of examples to offer out of his own experience. The lists always tend to include many examples of poor supervisors; that is, there is a tendency to personalize. The items do not come in any particular order, but the lists look something like this one:

1. Loud reprimanding in the presence of other people.
2. Favoritism toward certain individuals in the unit.
3. Insufficient knowledge of the work.
4. Poor instruction—either too general or not complete.
5. Deadlines not explained in advance.
6. Using employees as scapegoats for the supervisor's errors.
7. Refusal to admit mistakes.
8. Failure to support (and fight for) his people.
9. "Picky"—finds fault with everything his people do.
10. "Snoopervision"—always poking his nose into personal matters (usually explained as different from being *asked* for advice on personal matters).
11. Oversupervision, that is, too close watching of everything his people are doing.

12. Failure to delegate authority to his people, where needed.

13. Does not trust his people fully.

14. Gossips about one of his people with another in the same group.

15. Never gives credit where credit is due.

16. Failure to provide adequate materials or facilities for his people.

17. Clear-cut, prompt decisions almost impossible to get.

18. Treats his people as inferiors, not as associates.

19. Displays too much "brass"; never lets anyone forget he is the boss.

20. Never gives his people a chance (i.e., to get credit, to win promotions, to use their own initiative, etc.).

Some lists have run to as many as fifty to seventy-five items, with surprisingly little duplication. Actually, it is rare for a group of a dozen or more adults to list as few as the twenty items above. On the other hand, every one of the twenty occurs in almost every list.

Such lists as these have been published before,[1] but they are possibly of greatest value when placed where they may easily be seen every day by the supervisor who helped make one. After all, these are examples of things to be avoided. It is by such things that people judge their supervisors. And any set of principles purporting to be basic to supervision must take such examples as these into account.

We could at this point attempt to classify supervisors into a number of categories, although no useful purpose is served by doing so. It is worth our while, however, to distinguish between an autocratic leader and a democratic leader.[2] The autocrat we often call a "boss," which derives

1. For example, see Edward C. Kellogg, "The Top-Flight Supervisor: A Profile" in *Leadership on the Job—Guides to Good Supervision,* ed. Supervisory Management Staff of the American Management Association (New York, 1957), pp. 18–25.

2. Auren Uris has written an excellent article on this subject, which was reprinted in *Readings in Management,* ed. Max D. Richards and William A. Nielander (Cincinnati: South-Western Publishing Co., 1958), pp. 377–385.

from the Dutch *baas*, meaning master. He is the one who directs, commands, and controls the people over whom he has authority in such a way that no one ever forgets that he is indeed the *baas*. Such a boss frequently drives his people, uses his authority much like a whip, demands complete obedience from his "inferiors," and to a greater or lesser degree acts as a petty tyrant. This type believes that all his people have to do is what he tells them. In spite of dissatisfaction and hard feelings among his people, he is often able to get good production out of his group, although there is ample evidence to indicate that this production is not as great as can be had by less authoritarian means.[3]

Conversely, a democratic leader is one who uses little authority; who encourages his people to participate with him in getting the job done; who deals fairly and patiently with his people and with good humor; who treats his people as associates in a joint undertaking; and who obviously likes and is respected by the members of his group. Such a man or woman is seldom referred to as the "boss" except in a respectfully friendly way. We are inclined to think of him or her as a leader in the truest sense. Commonly, a democratic leader is successful in encouraging his people to exert the greatest and most intelligent efforts of which they may be capable. He, as with the boss's group, experiences dissatisfactions, but they are seldom bitter. It is a privilege and a pleasure to work with such supervisors. Some of them are great in the same sense that some teachers are great.

A number of different terms are used to designate supervisors. For example, a "manager" is a person who directs the work of an organization or a segment of it. Inevitably, he is a supervisor, since the work of any organization is per-

3. Rensis Likert, Director of the Institute for Social Research at the University of Michigan, has summarized a good deal of data on this point in "Developing Patterns in Management," American Management Association General Management Series 178: 32–51, 1955, and 182: 3–29, 1956. See also his book *The Human Organization: Its Management and Value* (New York: McGraw-Hill Book Co., 1967).

formed by people, and his direction must flow through them. Administrators, executives, directors are all supervisors, since their operations must always be carried out by other people. Foremen, of course, are supervisors. So is a "chief," a word much used in government to specify the head of a bureau, division, or branch. Terms such as these carry with them some additional ideas. People often associate mahogany desks and thick carpets with the term "executive." A foreman is often thought of as a supervisor in an industrial plant, or of unskilled labor, and so on.

Because these terms are in common use, many people tend to think that they have precise meanings and that everyone uses them alike. This is simply not a fact. All these terms have meanings that overlap a good deal, even though some books or authorities try to give them special meanings for special purposes.

What Supervisors Must Be Able to Do

Anyone working as a supervisor of people and a manager of work must learn how to do a number of things. We can list these as follows:

1. He must learn how to guide and direct the efforts of the people he is responsible for supervising. This involves learning about the many factors that motivate people, and understanding and using skillfully the principles and methods of supervision known to be effective. Chapters 2 through 7 deal with this subject.

2. He must learn how to work in the organization of which he and his people are a part. This implies that a supervisor must know something about the principles of organization and how an organization operates most efficiently. We treat this in Chapter 10.

3. He must learn how to train or teach people to do their jobs. He must be able to train people for jobs of greater responsibility. There is a discussion of this in Chapter 8.

4. He must learn how to speak and write clearly and effectively, and how to read and listen. There are techniques for doing all these, and they are often lumped under the term "communications." This comes in Chapter 9.

5. He must learn how to analyze work loads. Anyone trying to supervise people and manage resources has to be able to judge what a fair day's work is—or a week's work, or a year's work. If he can do this, he can come closer to judging whether he is overstaffed or understaffed. In addition, he needs to know how the various kinds of work should be assigned. This helps him to avoid using high-priced people on low-priced work, or the reverse. We come to this in Chapter 11.

6. He must learn how to make a plan of action or operation. Good planning is important in any job, but particularly so in management. Chapter 11 considers this.

7. He must learn how to schedule work, making a timetable for a plan and assigning priorities to the various jobs involved in it. This, too, is treated in Chapter 11, since a plan without a timetable is not really complete.

8. He must learn how to improve operating efficiency. This is the kind of thing that pays off in easier, less costly operation. The methods are discussed in Chapter 11.

Chapter 12 considers ways to solve problem cases. Chapter 13 deals with important books and magazines in the field of supervision and management.

2   *Basic Principles of Supervision*

Supervision is the art of working with a group of people over whom authority is exercised in such a way as to achieve their greatest combined effectiveness in getting work done. It is best performed in an atmosphere of goodwill and zestful cooperation on the part of all the people involved—including, of course, the supervisor. It is possibly one of the most difficult of all the arts, since it demands an ability to use successfully and almost intuitively those principles of human relations that have proved true with most people most of the time.

Experienced supervisors will recognize that there are no sure and certain rules for working with "people" in general. They know, with the wisdom born of experience, that human beings are individually unique, and that this individuality has always to be considered in developing working relations. With due regard for the uniqueness of individuals, however, there are certain general principles that are used by successful supervisors as guides in working with their people. Each principle involves some companion ideas that need to be understood in order to appreciate the guiding principle. These principles are set forth below, with a discussion of each. The order in which they are listed is not significant— all of them are important.

PRINCIPLE ONE

People must always understand clearly what is expected of them.

Ordinarily, when a new man starts to work, he is eager to know what sort of an outfit he is getting into and what he is supposed to do, that is, what his particular job is going to be. An experienced supervisor takes advantage of this initial interest. He knows that if he fails to get the new man off to a good start, it may take more time and harder work to do it later on. He also knows that possibly never again will his man be as receptive and eager to learn as he is in the very beginning. At any rate, every new man should find out *very soon* after he reports for work:

1. What the organization stands for; how it is organized; how it operates; what it does; something of its history; and the career policy it uses with its personnel.

Getting these ideas across is essentially an exercise in salesmanship. The intent here is to convince the new man that he has entered the best possible organization, containing the finest people, doing the most important work in the most enlightened and efficient way. People like to feel that their outfit is a good one. They will put their best efforts into something important. Pride of organization is a motivating force with many people. Belief in the importance of what their organization does lends prestige to their part in it.

2. What his particular job is; how his job is related to those of his fellow workers; what authority he has, if any; and who his supervisor is.

It is with this group of items that there is often a good deal of confusion, sometimes for many years. Even if the new man is started off correctly, it is important to review these items from time to time. In a way, almost everything a man does later on depends on his knowing who is the boss, and on his having a clear-cut understanding of what his job is and how it fits with related jobs.

3. Where he gets materials, supplies, or equipment he may need; where his place of work is; and what the working rules of the organization are. These last would include such things as when he gets paid, time of starting and quitting work, coffee breaks, lunch period, leave, and all the other various rules peculiar to his particular organization.

Possibly, these things go without saying. These are important; they should be given attention. Here the supervisor may not need to explain personally. Some of his people can—and will.

4. How the quality of his work will be measured.

5. How the quantity of his work will be measured.

Both items 4 and 5 need careful thought. It is discouraging indeed for any man to find out after he has been working for some time that the quality of his work is below par. It is equally discouraging to learn too late that he is not producing as much as the supervisor expected. Quality and quantity have to be understood *in advance*. Unless they are, there is likely to be argument about them when the man discovers he does not see eye to eye with his supervisor on either or both items.

There are, possibly, other things a supervisor would need to be sure his people know. For example, in certain government agencies and, indeed, certain industries, a new man has to learn about security rules if his work involves secret materials or activities. In any event, all such things require discussion between the supervisor and the new man. This discussion had better be planned for in a systematic way. If it is not, some items are bound to be overlooked or forgotten. This will not be the fault of the new man.

A good deal of the information a new man needs should be in written form. Many government agencies—but not all—have such things as these in writing, and so do some industries and businesses:

An organization chart.

The objectives and operating policies of the organization.

The history of the agency.

The career system the agency uses.

General office rules for all personnel.

Individual job descriptions and explanations.

Performance standards of quantity and quality.

Individual training outlines for each job.

Armed with a full set of materials like these, a supervisor

can do a much better and more complete job than if he has to remember it all. Organizations that are aware that people are their most important asset will have these items prepared and available. Some organizations put the first five items in an employee's handbook or orientation manual. Obviously, the last three items are individual in character.

PRINCIPLE TWO

People must have guidance in doing their work.

Guidance is a general word. To be specific, it includes such things as these:

1. Current information. No one should be expected to work in the dark. Everyone wants to know what is going on that may affect his work. It is up to the supervisor to see that new developments—things about to happen, things that have taken place—are fully and promptly told to all the members of his group. He can do this in meetings or staff conferences, that is, with all of his people at the same time. If he does the job with one of his people at a time, it takes him much longer, and the chances are the grapevine will beat him to it. News often gets twisted and distorted on the grapevine. The consequences of listening to wrong or partially wrong information can often be troublesome or even disastrous. A grapevine has its roots in poor supervisory practice; it flourishes best where supervisors are careless about keeping their people up to date.

2. Specialty information. In addition to news about developments, people need to see and study the latest and best technical or special information relating to their work. The latest theories, principles, materials, and knowledge concerning their particular specialties are important to any worker. This may seem to be overgeneralized for every kind of worker. Possibly, unskilled laborers could get along without such information, but a better shovel, a better way to dig a ditch, a better broom or machine for cleaning floors, better equipment for moving heavy objects, better know-how in any kind of work whatever—all such things may help to improve the productivity of the people and their interest in the work.

In the professional fields, it is obvious that no forester or engineer, no physicist, no doctor, lawyer, or economist, no specialist in any field can develop without study of new knowledge in his field. It may be true, of course, that the supervisor cannot personally provide all such information; in fact, it would be better if he did not try. But he has a responsibility for seeing that such knowledge is readily accessible and easily available; for studying his people to ascertain where each is strong and where weak; for encouraging and promoting study of the right kind. Principle Six considers this last point more completely.

3. Information on techniques. Techniques vary with the kind of job, and a thoughtful supervisor will do well to make himself a check list for each job he has in his unit. He must be sure that each of his people knows the best *methods* for getting his particular work done. Methods or techniques are somewhat different from knowledge about the work, although they tend to merge.

But there are often techniques that are by no means part of the special knowledge needed to perform a given job. For example, many professional people do not always know such things as these:

a. How to listen.
b. How to speak.
c. How to write.
d. How to read.
e. How to organize work.
f. How to schedule activities.
g. How to conduct a meeting.

There are many how-to-do-it items that can be listed for any particular job, and there are some, such as the first six above, common to many jobs. The point is that the supervisor needs to be alert to the necessity of helping his people to use the easiest and most efficient techniques known. He should not only be on the lookout for these better techniques, but he should be working with his people in a systematic way to develop them.

4. Personality improvement. Last of our guidance items, this one is perhaps the most difficult to effect. Making personality improvement suggestions requires skillful handling. Every human being *has* shortcomings, and almost everyone will admit that he is not perfect. But point out to a particular individual that he has a particular fault—and you may be in trouble. Frequently, the person will deny the charge with some heat, although sometimes he will surprise you by admitting it. He may be lazy, or slow, or too talkative, or moody, or short-tempered, or too hasty in making decisions, or what have you. The trouble frequently is that he may not admit it, even to himself. And yet, every man is entitled to help from his supervisor on his weak personality points.

A thoughtful supervisor sees to it that each of his people receives helpful encouragement—by one means or another—to overcome a personality fault that may stand in the way of full expression of ability. I know of no successful formula for providing this encouragement or guidance and for getting it accepted. Success seems to rest on (a) the recognition by the man that he has a fault, (b) prevention of too great discouragement about it, (c) development of a real desire to overcome it, and (d) constructive help and encouragement in conquering it.

Each of these points is important. Generally, the recognition of the fault by the man is the most difficult to achieve. Too hard pressure on this first point may make the discouragement almost a disaster when the recognition finally comes. Too great discouragement makes for difficulty in developing a desire to overcome the fault. Once these steps are taken, help in conquering the fault is much easier to give and more certain to be accepted. This is possibly similar to the method described by Alcoholics Anonymous to make a nonalcoholic out of an alcoholic. There is no question but that the method is successful more often than not; however, as the AA people describe it, their method depends on the acknowledgment or recognition or confession of weakness, without which there is little hope for progress. The technique of correction is worth close study, particularly in more difficult cases.

PRINCIPLE THREE

Good work should always be recognized.

Almost any experienced supervisor will agree readily enough that this is a good principle. He will tell you that such recognition should be as public as possible. He will tell you that people like to feel appreciated, and that they will work all the harder when their efforts are noticed and commended. But the supervisors will also tell you, almost in the same breath, that this can easily be overdone. The worst part of it is that fear of overdoing it frequently acts to prevent some supervisors from giving any praise at all.

Nevertheless, opinion surveys continue to indicate clearly and unmistakably that people consider recognition of good work a characteristic of good supervisors. They consider lack of ready recognition of good work characteristic of poor supervision. The question is: What is the best way to put this principle into effective, reasonable operation?

Listed below are some of the ways a supervisor can recognize the good work that many of his people perform. They are arranged in order, beginning with the simplest and easiest way of all:

1. *Tell* the man, on the spot, that he has just done a good job. Do this preferably in the presence of other people.

2. *Write* to him, promptly and explicitly, and see that a copy of the letter gets into his personnel folder. (Throughout the federal government, in many state governments, in many companies, and in some other organizations, a personnel file

is maintained for each individual in the organization. Such files can be of immense value as a repository for all the actions and records concerning each of the people working in the company or agency. Generally these files, even after many years, contain few or no letters of commendation of the sort we are describing here.)

At this point let me note that telling a man or writing to him costs little or nothing. These are the least expensive, but possibly most valuable, ways of according recognition. The items following contain the more expensive methods.

3. Give him a certificate of merit, of whatever type the organization uses—if it has one.

4. Give him a cash award or bonus.

5. Give him a medal or certificate plus a cash award.

6. Give him a raise.

7. Promote him to a better job for which he is qualified.

From this list it is obvious that the method of recognition must be tailored to the degree of excellence of performance and made in accordance with the policies of the organization.

But all this depends primarily on whether supervisors are intent on making the principle of recognition actually work. It is not necessarily true that the more awards there are, the better the supervision. But it does seem clear that the easy, simple methods of telling people or writing to people about their good jobs well done are basic supervisory techniques.

PRINCIPLE FOUR

Poor work deserves constructive criticism.

If it is true that good work deserves recognition, it seems equally true that poor work must also be appropriately recognized. This is an area in which most of us excel. It seems, somehow, far easier to criticize than to praise. It often seems easier to detect poor work than to detect good work. And yet, any man deserves (and usually expects) criticism of poor work that he has done (and that he recognizes to be poor).

Criticism should be given in private. Public censure of a man is compounded by the number of other people who see and hear him receive it. But it is not enough to confine criticism to private sessions between the supervisor and one of his people. The criticism must also be constructive.

One of the best ways to lower a man's satisfaction with his work, his interest in the job, and even his self-confidence, is to bawl him out. A good bawling-out may relieve a supervisor's feelings about a mistake or a poor job, and it may satisfy his ego, but it will most certainly not improve the productivity of his unit. A man who has been harshly criticized or unmercifully tongue-lashed may seethe for months over the incident. He may not get over it for a long time, possibly for years. His resentment may well find expression in doing less than he could do if he felt like it. Here again, opinion surveys among government as well as industrial workers show clearly that people simply do not consider supervisors top-ranking who are unnecessarily harsh in dealing with their people.

The supervisor's objective is to keep his people operating at their fullest possible capacity. When they do poor work, his task is to get them to do better, not to vent his dissatisfactions on them. The question is not who is to blame, but always how to improve his people's efforts.

PRINCIPLE FIVE

People should have opportunities to show that they can accept greater responsibilities.

Sooner or later every job in any organization will become vacant, and a new man will have to be put in it. The "head-scratching" method of filling an unexpected vacancy is a poor one. In contrast, any agency led by men of vision seeks to be ready to fill any and all vacancies whenever they occur. This requires that all supervisors take advantage of every opportunity to let their people show what they can do.

When the time comes for filling a vacancy, there is no need for uncertainty or head-scratching. The best men are already known, because they have been trained and tried. The only problem is to choose the best qualified. We are assuming here, of course, that simple seniority is not the criterion for promotion; rather, that the best-qualified people, regardless of age or sex or color, are given the opportunity to advance.

The grooming of people for positions of greater responsibility takes record-keeping. When a man has a chance to show what he can do, a good supervisor duly makes a note of how well the man performed, and files it in the personnel folder. The opportunities include special assignments to more difficult work or to other locations or offices. Supervisors' field trips or vacations provide other opportunities to leave men in charge. The whole point is to *plan* on developing people. Incidentally, the man who works steadily at his own improvement is more likely to bloom when he has the chance. This, too, a good supervisor encourages and carefully notes.

The testing of people before a full-fledged vacancy occurs is one way to avoid poor placement. It is not a positive guarantee, of course, because people change, but it does help materially to cut down the numbers of poor transfers or promotions. Putting untried people in jobs is not good management. And the supervisor who believes he has an unfailing ability to pick good men is due for some surprises.

So far, all of this is from the point of view of the organization and the supervisor. From the point of view of the people involved (and *all* of us in organizations are involved), the opportunity for advancement is one of the things they work for. Students fresh out of college always want to know what kind of career an agency can offer and what their opportunities are likely to be. No use telling them "When I was your age, I was glad just to have a job." This is the land of opportunity; the young man charting his course wants to know where he is likely to be in five or ten years or more.

Furthermore, when a man performs successfully in one job, he knows as well as his supervisor does, and as well as his agency or company should, that he deserves an opportunity in a more responsible job. He wants—and he may well deserve—more responsibility, higher salary, improved status.

Both from the standpoint of the organization and of the employees, then, a supervisor is well advised to take advantage of or create opportunities for his people to get ahead. Parenthetically, let me note that a supervisor who comes to be recognized as a developer of good men is likely to find his own advancement more rapid.

PRINCIPLE SIX

People should be encouraged to improve themselves.

For many years in America there has been all too common acceptance of the erroneous idea that when a man graduates from school, he is "educated." Whether from grammar school, high school, college, or university makes little difference except in degree. Your diploma becomes your passport, although it is recognized that college diplomas will get you into more places than high school diplomas. In a sense, these diplomas have come to be regarded as certificates of separation—of separation from all further education.

Such ideas have led Robert Blakeley to characterize American education as *terminal* in character.[1] As he sees it, "you are educated only if you ceaselessly continue to educate yourself"—a statement he once made to a college graduating class. And with such an idea, educators, scientists, men of affairs, leaders in professional fields, and well-educated people everywhere agree most heartily.

For eight, twelve, sixteen, or more years a man may receive intensive training in various subjects. The intent, generally, is to show him how to use his mental faculties for solving various kinds of problems. Most of the problems he deals

1. In *Adult Education in a Free Society*, a collection of speeches, ed. J. R. Kidd (Toronto, Canada: Guardian Bird Publications, 1958).

with in school are simulated or borrowed; they are not necessarily real, nor are they necessarily his own. When he leaves school, he begins to encounter problems in great variety, never considered or discussed in school. Generally, the more education he has had, the better equipped he may be to deal successfully with these new problems.

Education, to most Americans, almost always conjures up visions of a school building and classrooms. People speak of education as though it were a sort of commodity that is to be had if one goes to get it at the proper place. As Blakeley puts it, this kind of thinking enables us to say to each other: "I got my education at Podunk. Where'd you get yours?" In fact, our education is never finished, not until our lives end. There is nothing for it; either we continue our education and, thereby, our ability to solve new problems, or we stagnate. There is no middle course.

A man can improve his mind in many ways: by reading; by discussion, especially with people more able than himself; by expressing himself in writing; and in other ways. It is a wise supervisor who can so stimulate his people that they continue to be eager to learn, thirsty for knowledge, and alert for new and useful ideas. To so stimulate people requires great skill and thoughtfulness; many teachers are unable to do this, at least with all their students. And yet we are suggesting that where trained and experienced teachers may have failed, nevertheless, supervisors should try very hard. Those who succeed will find they have a group of people working with them who are going places, and who bring to their work such imagination and vision as may transform their daily tasks.

PRINCIPLE SEVEN

People should work in a safe and healthful environment.

Last of our "half-dozen" principles is this one, which is so often overlooked. Almost anyone will agree that this is a supervisory responsibility wherever, for example, the people in a unit make use of machinery or drive automotive equipment. There is recognition, too, of this responsibility where the people involved must do heavy physical work. But it is much less common to find supervisors who are well aware of the safety and health precautions necessary in an ordinary business office.

Any office has plenty of potential hazards. Tripping over light cords or open file drawers at the bottom of a cabinet, standing in front of doors that may be swung open unexpectedly, catching arms, hands, or legs on furniture edges or splinters, trying to move too-heavy furniture, slipping on waxed floors, electric fixtures in disrepair—all such simple situations can and do lead to serious accidents. Besides these, there are ventilation, lighting, and other problems in any enclosed work place that can become of major consequence. There are technical standards for these, all easily available from the National Safety Council. There are health hazards, too—for example, the overly conscientious worker who comes to the office with a severe and contagious cold—and these too require supervisory attention. Not everyone is as fully aware of safety and health hazards as he should be. If a supervisor does not pay attention to this matter, who will?

3 Supervisor's Expectations

A few years ago a social psychologist and an education specialist conducted an unusual experiment in a California elementary school.[1] They had reason to believe from previous studies that children in school might do better *if their teachers expected them to.*

The experimenters got the teachers to give a special intelligence test to their more than five hundred students. This test was not a new one, but it was unfamiliar to the teachers. They were told that the test could reveal children who were about to spurt ahead in their studies, or "bloom" scholastically.

After the tests had been collected, however, they were simply filed away and not used at all. Instead, the names of 20 percent of the students in the school were picked at random— or essentially, as the report puts it, drawn out of a hat. Their names were specially marked on class lists, which were turned over to the teachers. These marked names, the teachers were told, indicated the children who had scored high on the special test. They were the students who were about to spurt or bloom.

All the children in the school had been previously classified into groups or tracks, as is done normally in many of our schools—a fast track, a medium track, and a slow track— indicating, respectively, the students of high, medium, and low ability. But the names pulled out of the hat in the study were absolutely random, and so, mixed in the sample, there were students from the slow, the medium, and the high tracks. There was, in fact, no relation whatever between the special intelligence test the children had taken and their ability. Actually, the only difference between the "special" children

1. Robert Rosenthal and Lenore Jacobson, *Pygmalion in the Classroom* (New York: Holt, Rinehart and Winston, 1968).

and their classmates was *in the minds of the teachers.*

Now this was a rather ornery trick, if you like, and the researchers were a little concerned about deceiving the teachers. Long afterward, the deception was explained, and the teachers, instead of being angry, were pleased to have been part of an important social study.

At any rate, careful records were made of the children's IQs determined by usual tests both before the special test was administered and at intervals thereafter. The results were impressive. They were also statistically significant. The children *not* on the earmarked list gained an average of more than eight IQ points, but the children on the lists as "bloomers" gained more than twelve points. In other words, the selected children did 50 percent better than the unselected ones. And because their teachers expected them to spurt ahead, this is exactly what they did.

We should note here that other studies have shown that it is very difficult to increase IQ scores even with the most concentrated coaching. In the experiments described above, both the control group (unmarked) and the experimental group (the designated or marked children) increased their IQ scores significantly. The biggest improvements, though, were in the experimental group of children, and the conclusion is clear that the children did better if their teachers expected them to. This is what our two researchers had set out to check.

It is also interesting to note that the biggest gains were made by children in the first and second grades. In these grades one out of five undesignated children gained twenty IQ points or more, but of the special children, one out of two gained that much. There were other highly interesting results in this *Pygmalion in the Classroom* study. One was that the effects of teacher expectation began to show up within just a few weeks. Another was that the effects lasted afterward for periods ranging from a number of months up to nearly two years.

The experimenters did not know how the teachers may have communicated their expectations to the children, but they believe this must have been a matter of attitude. By the tone of voice, by the way the teachers looked at them, the children may have realized the teachers' confidence or expectation of them. Teachers may have paid greater attention to the selected children, been more pleasant, friendly, encouraging. Of course such attitudes also rub off on others—the unselected children—which would help explain the gains in IQ they made as well.

Rosenthal and Jacobson summarize numerous other studies that point in the same direction as their study. We may especially note one of these, performed by A. Bavelas. In his experiments foremen were led to believe that some of the women under their supervision had scored high on tests of intelligence and finger dexterity when actually they had gotten low scores. The foremen were told that others had scored low, when they really had scored high. The foremen did not know which women had scored high and which low, but *they thought they did*. In other words, the foremen, like the teachers, were deceived. Regardless of the high or low scores, however, if the foremen expected high performance, the production record of the women workers proved superior to that of other workers. And where the foremen expected low performance, they got just that.

A study by Gordon and Durea is cited in which "when examiners behaved more warmly toward their eighth-grade subjects, the IQ scores obtained were over six points higher than when they behaved more coolly toward their adolescent subjects."

They cite Crow, who found that college-age subjects performed better at a coding task if they were treated warmly. In other experiments, military personnel were more alert in detecting signals "when the experimenter was warmer, and less alert when the experimenter was cooler toward the subjects." And more warmly treated nursery school children scored nearly ten IQ points higher than did children who were treated with indifference. Other citations from the literature caused Rosenthal and Jacobson to conclude that "at least sometimes a subject's performance of an intellectual task may be unintentionally determined by the prophecy (or expectation) of the examiner."[2]

In recent years mounting evidence shows that where and when children are expected by their teachers to perform in a superior way, the children will do so, regardless of IQ and other tests that indicate that they will not or cannot. Conversely, if teachers expect children to respond in an inferior way, the children respond in that way, again regardless of other tests predicting better performance.

Altogether, the work may be summarized by the sentence that opens *Pygmalion in the Classroom*: "People, more often than not, do what is expected of them."

What Supervisors Can Expect

There are many constraints and misconceptions that operate to defeat supervisors. Possibly foremost among these is the business of *classifying people,* a common habit among us all. Everyone tends to put people in compartments or categories. We decide that a man is either bright and even brilliant, or else dull or outright stupid. He has talent, he is "gifted," or he has little or no talent. We carry this classifying into the classroom, as we have already seen, grouping students into fast, medium, and slow tracks. In college we may put them into A, B, C, D groups, or failures.

Most such classifications as these are supposed to relate directly to intelligence or brain power. But we also place

2. In addition to the studies of Rosenthal and Jacobson, the interested student will find it well worthwhile to read "Managing Motivated Employees" by W. N. Penzer of IBM in *Personnel Journal*, May 1971; also J. Sterling Livingston, "Pygmalion in Management," *Harvard Business Review*, July–August 1969; and David E. Berlew and Douglas T. Hall, "The Socialization of Managers: Effects of Expectations on Performance," *Administrative Science Quarterly*, September 1966.

people in fast, medium, or slow groupings for other reasons. The assumption is often made that if a person has a skin color other than white, he may prove to be less intelligent or possessed of less ability. Poorly dressed, unclean humans are often automatically classed in the slow track. Many studies by sociologists and psychologists have produced just such findings as these.

Scientific evidence indicates that we are often quite wrong in our assumptions and classifications. Besides the evidence coming from the work of Rosenthal, Jacobson, and many others, another important factor is often overlooked.

The fact is that every human being, regardless of race, color, or sex, receives at birth a human brain. This brain develops rapidly in the first few years of life. It is the most remarkable biological mechanism in existence. Our ability to perceive, to think, to reason, to learn, and to remember is built into the human nervous system with its ultimate directing center, the brain. This system is under genetic control; that is, human beings are *born* with an inherent capacity unmatched in any other organism.

The capacity of the human brain is fantastic. It contains more than a million million cells (or a trillion, or 10^{12} cells, if you like). The interconnections between these million million cells are more numerous than the cells themselves. We have no real idea yet how many cells and connections are involved in purely ordinary thoughts. We do know, though, that the brain we have is underutilized even by the most "brilliant" of humans. In an instant the brain can accept all the things that can be seen, felt, heard, smelled, or tasted, either individually or in any combination. It can evaluate these sensations or groups of sensations, decide upon those most likely to be prevailing, select with precision the motor units of the body that must thereupon be activated, then control and regulate the resulting required actions both quantitatively and qualitatively. The number and complexity of computations required to do this "ordinary" sort of thing is staggering. Compared to the human brain, our most highly sophisticated computers are scarcely more than toys.[3]

The human brain can store enormous numbers of facts and ideas. It can reproduce these in any combination instantly or after a long period of years. It can arrange an infinite number of combinations of facts and ideas, evaluate them, compare them with stored standards, and issue orally or in other ways the possible conclusions resulting from such study. It can do this at once, in a little while, or after a long time.

And *every normal, ordinary human being anywhere in the world can do this.* The most creative, imaginative, innovative, intelligent creatures on the face of the earth are the human beings—black, white, red, yellow, or brown—that inhabit it.

The capacity of the human brain is still far beyond the understanding of our foremost scientists. We have done little more than tinker with it. The more it is studied, the more the brain defeats our analysis. There are major segments of the brain whose functions are completely unknown. The pathways of thought astound us with their complexity. The crude studies of what happens when part of the brain is destroyed come nowhere near explaining what happens inside the brain with respect to ordinary perception, evaluation, judgment, and memory. The study of its operation is beset with technical difficulties that we are only beginning to resolve. It is not the brain of the so-called genius we are talking about here; it is every brain, the brain possessed by every normal human being.

What we are getting at here is the simple idea that instead of classifying human beings who possess this amazing brain, we had better address ourselves to methods aimed at getting it into full use. Instead of deciding in advance that any human being is slow, dull, stupid, or lacking in intelligence, let us

3. A more complete summary of our existing knowledge about the human brain is presented in *Biology and the Future of Man,* edited by Philip Handler, president of the National Academy of Sciences (New York: Oxford University Press, 1970), pp. 324–378.

take advantage of the remarkable power conferred on him by his inherited capacity for thought.

This thought leads us back to the idea expressed in the beginning of this chapter. What we expect of other people, we are likely to receive—without any particular limit as far as we know, since all humans possess what appears to be an infinite capacity—the human brain.

Supervisory Approach

With the foregoing ideas in mind, let us now consider how they may be applied to the situation of a supervisor with people under his direction. How can he use these ideas? Two major aspects of the matter are (1) clear awareness of the immense capacity of every human brain, and (2) expectation.

Interestingly, there is some highly important factual evidence concerning the results that can be attained through the application of these ideas. We turn, for example, to another field entirely, the work of the extraordinary Japanese violin teacher Shinichi Suzuki.[4]

Suzuki has been teaching the violin for more than thirty years. One day early in his career a father came into his studio with his four-year-old boy and asked Suzuki to teach the child to play the violin. Suzuki was uncertain; the child was too young; Suzuki had never worked with a small child before and was not at all sure that it could be done. But he agreed to consider the matter.

Suzuki says in his book that as he thought about the problem, it dawned on him that this little boy could, after all, speak Japanese. And Japanese, no less than any other language, is a difficult thing to learn. If the little boy could learn Japanese at this young age, surely he could learn other "difficult" things, such as to play the violin. So Suzuki began trying to teach the boy and was successful.

4. Shinichi Suzuki, *Nurtured by Love: A New Approach to Education* (New York: The Exposition Press, 1969).

He took on other youngsters. By now Suzuki has trained over 200,000 children from four to ten years of age to play fine music on the violin. He says he has never had a single failure. None of his pupils had to pass a test before entering the school. And these children became what we call accomplished musicians. They play classical music written for the violin, and they play it well.

We may take the word of the great cellist Pablo Casals on the excellence of Suzuki's pupils. When Casals was in Tokyo he heard four hundred children, aged five to twelve, play their violins and was moved to tears by their skill.

Suzuki believed that any child has a virtually unlimited capacity, and he confidently expected each child to develop into an accomplished musician. And as he worked skillfully to develop the inherent talent he was sure was there, he succeeded.

Whether a student liked or disliked music or playing the violin is beside the point. All Japanese children don't necessarily like the Japanese language, but they learn it just the same. "Ability grows as it is trained," Suzuki says. If there are failures, it is the teacher who has failed, not the student. The time may come, the great teacher suggests, when not a single student will fail in school.

Of equal importance, Suzuki notes that "if you compare a person who practices five minutes a day with one who practices three hours a day, the difference—is enormous. Those who fail to practice sufficiently fail to acquire ability.

"Superior ability," he goes on to say, "can be produced in anyone."

What can a supervisor do with such ideas? Are they practical? Bavelas' study with the foremen suggests that these ideas are indeed practical. But note that their usefulness depends on the sincere and honest belief of the supervisor that all of his people can prove to be outstanding employees. He cannot disguise his true feelings by hearty but insincere encouragement. His underlying feelings, if they are negative, will inevitably be communicated to his people by his attitude and will give him away.

For such a reason, this discussion is somewhat detailed. Supervisors need to understand the enormous capacity of the human brain—*any human brain*. They need to know with certainty that the people under their supervision—fast, medium, or slow people—are alike in the capacity they have for excellence. Supervisors need to realize that their real problem is not to replace people with others classified as better or superior, but rather to undertake the most skillful efforts of which they are capable to unleash and improve the abilities of the people they already have. They have before them the potential; it is up to them to help give it expression.

One last point needs to be made. Suzuki worked with children; so did Rosenthal and Jacobson. In the San Francisco school it was the youngest children who made the greatest gains. Suzuki, in fact, once turned down an offer to work in a new school dealing entirely with adults. He preferred not to do "repair work," as he said, but rather to work with relatively unspoiled youngsters. Are we to assume that it is too late to expect improvement in the adults with whom supervisors must ordinarily work?

It is by no means too late. Numerous studies have shown clearly enough that the responses of adults are quite similar to the responses of children. We have already noted Bavelas' work with women, who were adults, and the experiments with military personnel and college students. In the study of corporation executives by Livingston, and of managers by Berlew and Hall,[5] the men concerned were all adults. These few studies are supported by many others. They may serve to remind us of something Adlai Stevenson once said in the United Nations Assembly. He remarked, "Children don't grow older, they just grow taller."

But there is another aspect to the adult problem that is of great importance. This is the fact that the first year in an

5. See Berlew and Hall's study, already cited.

organization is a very critical period for any new recruit. When people enter a company or an agency for the first time, they come into it much the same as children entered Suzuki's studio. Almost everything is new. If they are trained correctly from the very beginning in this new situation, then little "repair work" is needed later on. "Never again will he [the new man] be so . . . ready to learn as he is in his first year."[6] The moral of all this is, then, for supervisors to undertake the best training program they can devise, and to put it to work with their new people from the very first day.

6. Berlew and Hall.

4   Some Techniques in Supervising

The skill with which you go about supervising comes only with practice. *How* to supervise, how to put the principles of supervision into practice, make up the art of supervision. We take up now a few ideas that may prove of value to you as a supervisor. They are not guaranteed to work with everyone, nor in every situation. But experienced and able supervisors have often found them to be of considerable value.

1. *How to Begin Supervising*

Assuming that you are new at the job of supervising, one way to start is to *learn all you can about your people.* This idea could well be listed as a principle of supervision, as indeed it has been in some books and pamphlets on the subject.

If you must guide and work with people, it follows at once that you will need to know a lot about them in order to do a good job of it. You should know about their background, their schooling, their philosophy, their habits, their attitude toward their work, their ambitions, something of their family and social life, and so on. This may seem to be a big order, and it is clear that you can never know everything about every person you supervise. But you ought to know enough to be reasonably sure what each of them is likely to do in a given set of circumstances, and how each is likely to react to your guidance. How you learn all this is up to you. A wise supervisor learns what to look for, when to ask direct questions, when to avoid questions, and when to listen. A poor supervisor is likely to judge people too quickly, to catalog them without study.

An important idea to keep in mind as you work with your people is that each person is different from every other person. We all say this to each other, but we still tend strongly to classify people into types characterized by a single factor of personality. Many of us tend to classify people by their "looks"; e.g., anyone looking like the Hollywood or television version of a gangster is not to be trusted! All this is unwise. People should be judged by what they do, how they think, how they act; they should not be prejudged by formula or popular misconception.

Scientifically speaking, people *are* different. As you may read in *The Human Animal* by Weston LaBarre, each of two individual parents contributes to his offspring an average of some thirty thousand genes, or inheritance factors. The number of possible sets of thirty thousand genes donated by each parent is two multiplied by itself thirty thousand times. The number of possible combinations that two parents can produce is two multiplied by itself sixty thousand times. (Two multiplied by itself only twenty-nine times will give you a figure of over a billion. Try it!) Then consider that each individual human being also has had a unique set of experiences that have helped to make him what he is. As LaBarre points out, all the human beings who have ever lived have simply not scratched the surface of the number of possible varieties in the human species. Recent discoveries, incidentally, indicate that the number of genes may be far greater than LaBarre's thirty thousand.

Besides this, remember that you see your people only part of the time. Their homes, their families, their hobbies, their recreation are also of great importance to them. You may see them eight hours out of twenty-four, and five days out of seven; but this is not the major portion of their lives. Your people are *whole* human beings; they are not just employees of your unit of organization.

On the basis of what you learn about each of the whole, unique human beings whose work you are to direct, you can proceed with increased confidence as you come to understand each one. All this does not mean that no two individuals will ever react the same way in a particular situation. The fact is that human beings do react similarly under certain conditions, as we shall see in later chapters. Principles of supervision are based on this fact. But individuals are more likely to respond to your guidance if you treat them as individuals, not as workers or employees or subordinates.

2. *How to Give Orders*

An expert supervisor seldom finds it necessary to give an order to his people in the form of a direct *command*. As a supervisor you have that authority, of course, and there may be times when nothing else would be effective, but these times ought to be rare. The best way of all—and the one requiring greatest skill—is to help your people analyze a situation in such a way that the situation itself gives the order. Both you and your people can frequently agree on the wisest course of action. This is the order, which you will be expected to state clearly as the course of action "we" should take. Orders of this kind are almost always carried out more intelligently than an unexplained command.

These are the two extremes: direct commands versus mutual agreement on needed action. In between are a number of other ways of giving an order. They depend on the situation and on the individual. If possible, try for agreement on the best course of action. If this does not or cannot work, try suggesting. If your man is slow to pick up suggestions, then try asking. If there is no other alternative, then you may have to use a direct command.

3. *How to Get Help from Your People*

There are many ways of doing a job. You can do everything of any importance yourself. Or you can pass in advance on

everything any of your people want to do. In either case
you may be able to get the job done. In both cases, you will
probably get stomach ulcers eventually, and you may wonder
why you are always having to replace people who are leaving your outfit. You will be, to put it mildly, a rotten supervisor.

The people under your guidance are there to do a job.
Eventually, as you acquire skill, you will let them do it. Bas-
ing your actions on how well you know your people, you
will judiciously delegate authority to make decisions and to
act. Systematically, you will make certain that what you want
done is done the way you want it. Gradually, as you work
with your people to help them get the work done, you will
find them referring to you for help whenever they really
need it, at the right time, and in the right way. As your
confidence in your group grows, you will at last begin to
experience the warm, fine feeling a topnotch leader gets from
guiding a loyal, hard-hitting, capable bunch of people. It
may even be said that you seem to have a soft job because
your people seem to be doing all the work!

4. *How to Make Decisions*

Over and over again, your people will expect you to make
decisions about the work. They will try, and they should, to
influence your decisions; they will lay many facts or opinions
before you; they will help you make the decisions. In the
end, though, it is up to the supervisor to decide.

When a definite decision is called for, make it as promptly
as possible. Be sure you know whether you have the authority to make it. You can *never* get all the facts, but be sure
you have all the facts you *can* get that bear on the matter. Be
sure you have weighed the facts you have, and have sorted
the really important ones from the lesser ones. Then decide
—and make it stick.

People will excuse a mistake now and then, but they will

seldom excuse a man who never makes a clean-cut decision. An otherwise good supervisor may be lost if he dilly-dallies. He will be doubly lost if he changes his decisions to suit the ideas of the last person to see him. Calm, thoughtful consideration of a problem in all its facets, followed by a logical, reasoned decision, is a sure way to the establishment of confidence.

5. *How to Criticize*

When you praise people, you should do it publicly if you possibly can. And conversely, when you must criticize or reprimand people, do it privately, *never* in the presence of a man's fellow workers. These are aspects of two major principles of supervision discussed in Chapter 2.

When you do criticize, it is usually good business to start out by telling a man what you like about his work. Then tell him what you do not like. Always tell him why, and always do it in a friendly way, with due regard for the situation. The point is, if your man gets the idea you are really trying to help him, he will be likely to take your criticism to heart. If you only make him sore, or if he does not understand your criticism and thinks it unfair, your criticism will not be worth much. Finally, be ready with a suggestion on what the man can do to redeem himself.

People usually know when they deserve criticism. If they do not get it, they may lose a certain amount of respect for their supervisor. Timeliness, therefore, is important in criticizing. Incidentally, it pays to avoid ridicule when you criticize, except under very special circumstances and when you know exactly what you are doing. All during the time you are criticizing a man for anything, keep in mind that the *dignity* of people is important to them. A man always deserves a chance to save face.[1]

1. You may find it interesting to read George Heaton, "The Dignity of the Individual," in *Readings in Management*, ed. Max D. Richards and William A. Nielander (Cincinnati: South-Western Publishing Co., 1958), pp. 75–81.

6. *How to Settle Grievances*

Three things are important here: (a) to be careful to get all the facts you can about the grievance; (b) to get both sides, if two people or factions are involved; and (c) to settle the matter as promptly as possible. If you do not have the authority to settle things, get help from your own supervisor.

You should never ignore a grievance, no matter how trifling it may seem to you. Petty grievances have a way of growing into tough problems. Let your man with a grievance air it completely; encourage him to talk fully about it. Sometimes the talking helps to settle it. Bear in mind that your final decision must be fair, impartial, and well understood by all concerned.

7. *How to Deal with the Problem Child*

Sooner or later, every supervisor gets a man in his unit who is lazy, opinionated, tactless, too slow, too fast, too talkative, moody, possessed of a persecution complex, nervous, unable to get along with other people, disloyal, discourteous, always late, never prepared, an apple-polisher—or who has some other fault that is extremely annoying or that disrupts the work generally.

Many people have the idea that the best way to deal with a problem child is to get him transferred somewhere else. But a personnel problem can rarely be solved this way. Where two personalities clash violently, a transfer may often be necessary; otherwise, the best place to deal with a personnel problem is right where it comes up.

Each problem is different and must be met and solved on the basis of its own characteristics. Avoiding problems like these is the distinguishing mark of a poor supervisor. Attacking such problems always requires that you gain the man's confidence first. If you are reasonably sure you have it, then here is one way to proceed that is often successful:

a. As soon as you are sure of your ground, talk to the man about his fault. See if you can find out the reason for it. Be sure you explain clearly what the man's fault means to you, to him, and to the organization. Get him to see it; then see if you can get him to tell you how he expects to overcome it. Agree with him on a course of action, which should include your own sympathetic help whenever needed. Then tell him, later on, how well he is doing.

b. If the first talk fails, try again after a reasonable interval. Go over the situation again. Search for more reasons. Try to get him to promise to do better, and to agree on the steps he will take. Follow it up again; praise him for any progress he makes.

c. If his fault persists and is getting serious, call him in again and go over the same ground once more. This takes patience, but do it with care. Then begin to consider his rating, the effect on his opportunities, job, salary, family, and so on. Be clear about this and try to gain his cooperation.

d. If there is still no progress, talk it over with your own supervisor and try to agree on a course of action. For example, the man may be warned that continuation may cost him his job—if things are that serious. He may be given a certain time in which to correct his fault. It may be considered with him whether he would do better in some other type of job, possibly in another organization altogether. These more rigorous steps usually should not be taken until there is pretty sure support "up the line."

In going forward in such a manner as this, start keeping notes about the time you reach the third step—you can simply remember the earlier stages. You may need notes of this kind later. But do not keep a "black book," whatever you do. Again, be sure you have all the facts you can get, and go at the job in a manner that will convince the man that you want to help him. Always follow through, and never make threats you cannot carry out.

8. *How to Deal with Misconduct*

Once in a long while, a supervisor may be confronted with a suspected or clear case of misconduct or serious irregularity. These cases may range from drinking on the job, neglect of duty, or refusal to do certain kinds of work, all the way up to theft, bribery, or criminal action. What to do in such cases depends on the circumstances, of course, but there are a few things any supervisor ought to know about such matters.

In the first place, an employee action that may prove serious enough to warrant his discharge, or that may land him in jail, is not something a supervisor can handle by himself. In most government agencies and many industries, supervisors do not have the authority to fire anyone; this is reserved to the highest authorities. It is important, therefore, that you get in touch with your supervisor. The two of you need to discuss the situation and decide what to do. An obvious decision might be to call in the personnel staff people of your organization for a consultation. This should not mean that you thereby wash your hands of the case. On the contrary, it is *your man,* and you carry an important responsibility with respect to the handling of the case. You know, or should know, the most about the man. You should, by all means, undertake to see the case through, insofar as your supervisory authority extends. Your recommendations should bear due weight with whatever authority makes the final decision.

In dealing with serious cases, it is of grave importance that you be sure about the facts involved. Obviously, you cannot delay indefinitely while you keep on checking. The point is that you should be in possession of sufficient information to justify whatever action you decide to take. When you intend to accuse a man of serious misconduct, you had better know where you stand. Once you are on firm ground, then act promptly.

If the situation demands immediate action, you can, in

most government agencies and in some companies, (a) order the man to stop work while you get in touch with your supervisor, or (b) order him to go with you to your supervisor, or (c) order him to go home while you check possible next steps with your supervisor. If the man refuses to obey orders, this is classed as insubordination, and would be taken into account later when a penalty is prescribed. These statements cannot be made here with any degree of finality, because different organizations have different ideas about what authority their supervisors may exert. For this reason, you had better know what your authority is—a long time ahead of any need for action.

In terms of the many thousands of people who are at work, the number of cases of real misconduct that turn up is small. The chances are rare that you will ever have to deal with one during your entire career. Notice, however, that petty matters have a habit of growing serious, and that misconduct is as preventable as accidents.

9. *How to Deal with Inefficiency*

There could be many reasons for inefficiency on the part of one of your people, but there is seldom an excuse for failure on your part to deal with it promptly and effectively. Over and over again, with monotonous regularity, tough personnel problems develop in which it turns out that a man has been getting a satisfactory performance rating although he has been inefficient all along.

Many supervisors instinctively recoil from dealing with inefficient employees on an honest basis. Telling a man he is not doing as good work as he should be can be unpleasant, if you want to make it so. If you can approach it openly and objectively, with an obvious interest in helping the man, however, the task can often prove to be unexpectedly pleasant. People usually appreciate help, even though some of them may at first refuse to believe they need it. To see a man improve his work as a result of your guidance is a gratifying experience a good supervisor will cherish for a long time.

We are assuming here that you have made full use of the principles of supervision outlined in Chapter 2. Your man knows exactly what is expected of him, and how much high quality work he should be turning out. You have done everything you could to keep him informed and have given him far more than ordinary help with his problems. You have pointed out his failings and worked with him to correct them. You have praised him for the things he does best. You have consulted your own supervisor and used up all the suggestions he could make. But in spite of considerable effort on your part, and perhaps on his as well, over a reasonable period, he is still unable to do his job well enough to be considered a satisfactory employee. Then, *and only then,* it may be proper to try these steps:

a. Discuss the whole problem in its entirety with your own supervisor. Be objective in your appraisal of the situation, and with your supervisor's help try to determine (1) whether your supervision of the man has been good enough, or (2) whether he is really an unsatisfactory employee. Be honest about this. You may not have succeeded for either of these reasons. It may be that the man deserved a trial under another supervisor. If he does, proceed accordingly. If not—

b. You, and possibly your supervisor, should talk the matter over with the man in a way that will convince him, if at all possible, of your fairness and genuine interest. It may be that he should get into some other kind of work. If so, undertake to help him find it, and enlist the help of the personnel office (if he is willing).

c. If your man is unwilling to cooperate—and some will be —then follow through with the procedure set forth in your instructions on dealing with cases of this kind. (All supervisors should know what these instructions are; they vary with the organizations.) In doing this, be sure you are in full possession of all pertinent facts and are fully justified in your action. Be prepared to follow through; and if dismissal or demotion is the action to take, and if the man appeals to higher authorities, which he has the right to do, be able to come forward with a clear, objective justification for your recommendation.

10. *How to Handle Long-Distance Supervision*

In many organizations, the supervisor is stationed a long distance away from the men he is expected to supervise. This makes supervision more difficult both for the men and for the supervisor. Usually, the greater the distance, the more difficult it is.

I have never found an equal substitute for talking with a man face to face. On the telephone and by mail, too many ways of conveying ideas are lost that are used in personal discussion. Simple gestures, expressions, tones of voice, and the like are often as important as what is said. Nevertheless, if your people are at a distance, there are various expedients available; and all of them depend for their success largely on how systematically they are used. Some of these are:

a. *Work plans.* The only satisfactory way for you to know what your people intend to do is to get from them a written plan. The plan can be simple, and it can be made for a period no longer than between your visits—or it can be made by months, quarters, or on a yearly basis. The plans should be changed as often as necessary, but they are a very important source of information for you. By using them you can give guidance when needed. For long-distance work they are almost mandatory.

Note that the plans must be your people's, not yours. *They* should make them and follow them. If you formalize them too much, and require too many things to be in them, they may easily become a burden. Plans are only statements of intention and should be used accordingly.

b. *Meetings.* You will need to hold meetings of your people at regular intervals—with due regard for travel costs, travel time, and interruption of regular work. These meetings will demand thoughtful and careful planning on your part and on the part of your people, so that the time you have is used in the most profitable way. Your people ought to know when they are to be held a long time ahead, so that they can plan their work.

These meetings make possible a review of recent work and discussions of plans for the next period. Here also can be arranged the special training you may want your people to have. In meetings, you have one of two possibilities for working face to face with your people. Use these meetings as valuable tools, never as unplanned, semisocial get-togethers. (Develop the social angle in the evenings.)

c. *Regular visits.* As often as the load of work permits, and as regularly as possible, you will need to visit each of your people at their work location. Your people should know, well in advance, when you are coming. They can then store up problems against the time and plan their own activities sensibly. When you get there, stay long enough to do an adequate job. Encourage your people to prepare for your visit and to be clear about the kind of help they want. Plan also what you want to get done.

The practice of dropping in unexpectedly, upheld by many people, is unsound. It not only makes it impossible to use time to best advantage, but it tends to build distrust and even fear, not confidence. *Always* write or phone when you cannot be there at your regular time. This is only ordinary courtesy expected from anyone.

d. *Reports.* If your meetings and visits are sufficient to maintain good communications, you may not need to ask for reports. Certainly you will do well to avoid them if you can. If they prove to be necessary, then by all means keep them as simple as possible. A weekly letter may often serve admirably, provided your men know pretty well what information you want. If your people are required to make reports by other offices of your organization, by all means use these yourself to avoid having your people do double work.

e. *Other devices.* Long-distance supervision almost forces the development of manuals or handbooks of some sort, in which procedures, policies, standards, methods, or other matters are clearly set forth. Sometimes, these are overdone, but they are valuable if they are used with common sense.

In April 1927 an experiment with human beings got under way at the Hawthorne Plant of the Western Electric Company at Chicago. This experiment, plus some others, and their surprising results have had a profound influence on the whole field of management and supervision for many years. They have been called a breakthrough in management.

The stated objective of this experiment was to find answers to such questions as these:

1. Do employees actually get tired out?
2. Are rest pauses desirable?
3. Is a shorter working day desirable?
4. Why does production fall off in the afternoon?
5. How do employees feel about the company?
6. What effects would changes in working equipment have?

To make the study, six experienced "female operators" were chosen to be the guinea pigs. Two of the girls, who were friends, were asked to select four other girls. These girls worked at the job of putting together a telephone relay. Each relay took about a minute to put together. All day long, day after day, the girls assembled about thirty-five small parts and secured them in position with four machine screws. This was monotonous, repetitive work, and it is not surprising that the research men wondered whether fatigue played a part in production.

The experiment began simply enough. The girls were invited to the superintendent's office, and the test was explained to them. They were willing to take part in it, but the record notes that they were shy at the first conference. During the first two weeks, then, a record was kept of the production of each girl, that is, of the number of relays she put together per hour, per day, and per week. The average was about 2,400 per week. The research men kept the record by means of an ingenious electric counting device that punched a hole in a traveling paper tape every time a girl put a finished relay in the chute alongside her bench. Also, in this two-week period, the girls were given complete physical examinations. According to the physician's report, they were "six normally functioning organisms."

Two weeks after the study began, the girls were moved into a special experimental room, which was simply a corner of the regular shop room, closed off by partitions. Temperature and humidity readings were made every hour, and a test observer made notes of remarks made by the girls and of anything else he thought significant. And for five weeks nothing else was done. The girls went on assembling parts, and the electric recorder mechanically noted how many they finished. The idea was to get the girls used to the new conditions.

After five weeks the experimenters made a change. Each girl had formerly been paid so much per relay, based on the average piece rate for about a hundred workers in the big shop. The change was to a new rate based on that of her own little group in the experimental room. This meant that each girl could earn an amount more nearly in proportion to her own individual efforts. Nothing else was changed for two months. During this time the girls produced relays a little faster than they had before. In the records maintained by the company, this was called Period Three. During Period Three, output was up slightly.

At this time the more significant experimental work was begun—or so the research men believed. They gave the girls two rest pauses of five minutes each, one at ten in the morning, one at two in the afternoon. These breaks were discussed with the girls—this was a regular practice all during the tests—and they thought five-minute pauses would be better than ones of ten or fifteen minutes. If the pauses were too long, they felt, it might be hard to make up the lost time. This change seems simple now that the coffee break is such a common custom in America, but at the time, it was unusual. This was Period Four, lasting for five weeks. Production definitely went up.

In the next period, the rest pauses were lengthened to ten minutes each. The change lasted a month, and during that time the daily and weekly output went up—higher than it ever had before.

Next, in Period Six, the girls got six rest periods a day for five minutes each. The research men kept this up for a month, but the girls did not like the constant interruption, and their output fell off slightly.

In Period Seven, the pauses were changed to a fifteen-minute morning break and a ten-minute afternoon break. In addition, the company provided refreshments. Production went up again and stayed up for the eleven weeks of this period.

Following this, the experimenters continued these same pauses, but changed some other conditions. They stopped work half an hour earlier each day. Production went up. Then they stopped work a full hour earlier each day. Rates of production went up, although the total fell off slightly. Later, the work week was cut from five and a half days to five days. The daily output increased, but the weekly output was slightly down.

The research men began to wonder what was happening. It seemed to them (as it may have to you) that no matter what they did, the girls continued to produce more and more and more. They began to wonder. Then they decided, with the full concurrence of the girls, on a bold and conclusive stroke. They would return to the beginning—no rest periods, no refreshments, no shortened hours. Obviously, production should fall to what it was in the beginning. This was supposed to be a scientific experiment; all the conditions were apparently clear and controlled; production, therefore, should be related to the experimental conditions introduced.

It is to the credit of Western Electric researchers that they decided on this return to original conditions. After all, some of their questions had been answered: rest pauses were obviously desirable; so were shorter working days. But at any rate, in September 1928, eighteen months after the tests had begun, everything was changed back to what it had been in the beginning. The research men felt that production should have dropped also, back to about what it was to start with.

Instead, *production rose to a point higher than it had ever been before,* and stayed that way for three months.

With a certain doggedness the experimenters pushed ahead. In the next period they went back to the fifteen-minute break in the morning and the ten-minute break in the afternoon. But this time the girls had to provide their own refreshments. Production climbed to even greater heights. During this period the girls were assembling three thousand relays a week—25 percent more than they had been producing to start with, and the output was steady and continuous.

One gains the impression that the research men were considerably puzzled over the continual increase in production. Their reports spoke of the "astonishing" upward trend in output, regardless of the kinds of changes introduced. Improvements in output were to be expected as a result of the rest pauses; after all, the work *was* monotonous, and breaks should have helped relieve the monotony. But how explain that the return to monotony, which should have resulted in a decrease in output, instead resulted in a new high in production?

The answer to the question turned out to have nothing much to do with the rest pauses, or the shortened hours, or refreshments. It had to do instead with a change in mental attitude of the "female operators." This came about as a result of two or possibly three major changes that were overlooked in the beginning. The first of these was that the experimental room was put in charge of an interested and sympathetic chief observer, who replaced the gang boss the girls were used to. The chief observer was interested in each girl and her output; and furthermore, his attitude convinced the girls of his interest and pride in their achievements. The clincher for this point lies in a remark made by one of the girls: "I hope I never see a gang boss again," said she. "We don't have to worry about getting bawled out about our rates up here."

The change from gang boss to chief observer meant a complete change in supervision. This was a major difference in itself. But there is more to it than that. The new supervisor—the observer—was *not* under the direction of the regular plant organization, as the gang boss had been. He was directed by the research group, to whom he was responsible. Further, the group of six girls was physically cut off from the rest of the company organization by the walls of the experimental room. All this was, in fact, an organizational change of great significance, although it has not been generally recognized as such. In recent years, from other research, we have learned that a simple change in supervisors—whether through training of the man or replacement by another— will not necessarily effect any great change in the group supervised. What must also occur is the right kind of a change in the organization above him that will give him the freedom to operate in an enlightened way. If both supervisory and organizational changes are made in such a way as to complement each other, then changes in production, morale, and so on, can be effected.

The third important change that had been introduced was that the various experimental changes were discussed in advance with the girls. At first, the girls were shy and uneasy, suspicious of the executives whom they were meeting. Later on, they gained confidence and spoke out frankly, as they found their ideas listened to and used. For the first time in their working lives these girls were being treated as human beings instead of "female operators." And also for the first time, they were *participating* in the planning of their own work. It seemed that when you treat people as human beings, they respond as human beings. And when they play a part in planning their own work, they outdo themselves in executing it.

These three changes in supervision, organization, and participation supplement and complement each other. Each must take place if the others are to be effective. Possibly this illustrates the need for coordination—that is, for a working together—of many factors, if the management is to be the best we can achieve. Here, however, we need to look a little further into the idea of participation and to consider how we can make use of it.

The experiments at the Hawthorne Plant went on for five years. The conditions of Period Seven, with the fifteen-minute break in the morning and the ten-minute break in the afternoon, were carried on as standard for the group. High output was maintained all this time, so that any excitement over the tests was clearly lost. The research men felt, as the years passed, that something permanent had been achieved. And so it had.

Participation at the Lincoln Electric Company

In 1895 the Lincoln Electric Company went into business making and repairing electric motors in John Lincoln's basement in Cleveland. Twelve years later James Lincoln, John's younger brother, joined the company. In 1914 James became the general manager of the business, which was still small and in poor shape financially.

One of the first things James Lincoln did was to get all the people in the company together. He asked them to elect representatives from each department to an advisory Board. This group was to provide him with advice and counsel on how best to run the company. Lincoln had the idea that if he could get all the employees to want the company to succeed as badly as he did, there ought to be no limits to what they could do together. This Board was purely advisory. Lincoln ran the company, but he listened to the Board's ideas and suggestions. Since that time, the Advisory Board has met twice every month.

This innovation was made at the beginning of the First World War. During that war, Lincoln Electric developed arc welding, not just for repair purposes, but for factory production of machinery and equipment. Later, in World War II, arc welding made possible the production of the Liberty ship fleet. Lincoln has specialized in this field ever since, and has now become the largest manufacturer of arc-welding equipment in the world.

But to get back to the development of the business:

In 1915 the company gave each employee a paid-up life insurance policy.

In 1919 the employees formed an association to provide for health benefits and social activities.

By 1923 every employee was getting a two-week paid vacation.

In 1925 the employees were able to buy stock in the company.

In 1929 the Board of Directors set up a suggestion system.

In 1934 the company began distributing bonuses to employees from profits remaining after taxes and relatively conservative dividends. Each employee received a check, the size of which depended on the quality of his performance during the year. The average bonus was about 30 percent of an employee's earnings for the year, which are about average for the Cleveland area. In the thirty-one years following, Lincoln Electric paid out $126 million in bonuses to its people.

During the ten years following 1934, a whole series of other ideas was set in motion. A pension plan was set up, paid for by the company; by 1964 the company had purchased retirement annuities for all employees at a cost of $13 million. A policy of guaranteed employment was established and followed. A merit rating plan was developed for deciding on each person's share of the bonus. Promotion from within was established as a policy. A job evaluation procedure was set up to determine rates of base pay. All the foregoing ideas have been carried on since their inception. Many of them came from suggestions made by the Advisory Board.

During the period of thirty years from 1934 to 1964, the Lincoln Electric Company experienced some great increases in their costs of manufacturing. For the principal materials used in the making of arc-welding equipment, the cost of steel increased 300 percent; the cost of copper went up 377 percent. Moreover, the cost of labor rose to a figure that was 547 percent above its cost in 1934.

In view of these increasing costs, it is natural to expect that the price of the arc-welding equipment must have gone up in proportion—up, say, to 300 or 400 percent of the 1934 prices. Instead, the company has been able to *reduce the cost of its product by 20 percent.*

A final indication of the success of Lincoln Electric policies may be seen in the monthly rate of separation, or turnover rate, of the employees. Since 1945 the turnover in all industry has been eight to ten times that of the turnover at Lincoln Electric. The rate in 1959 for all industry was 3.3 percent; for Lincoln it was 0.33 percent. This means that, on the average, industry was losing better than three workers out of a hundred each month, whereas it took nine months for Lincoln Electric to lose three workers.

A number of factors have been at work in this situation:

1. All the employees have participated in the running of the company through their representatives of the Advisory Board, and through their active suggestion system.

2. All the employees have profited from both their ideas and suggestions and the efficiency of their work. The profits have taken concrete form in bonuses, life insurance, pensions, paid vacations, health benefits, and the dividends from stock purchases.

3. No employee has had to fear a layoff; job security has

depended on his own efforts, not on factors over which he had no control.

4. Promotion has depended on a man's efforts. He could count on competition with associates rather than with people with influence brought into the company from outside.

James Lincoln believed that the full-fledged participation or cooperation of the entire working staff of the company accounts for its remarkable successes. He noted:

Cooperation is the working together of all people in the organization. . . . It means the enthusiastic *finding* of new methods, new tools, new ideas, by all people, from top to bottom in the organization. . . . Cooperation means the enthusiastic *use* by all people in the company of their best ideas, skills, and methods to reduce costs and improve quality. . . .[1]

Lincoln believed that the money incentive (i.e., bonuses) alone does very little to gain the cooperation of workers. The worker must be sure that his greater efficiency will indeed bring him greater rewards both in cash and in other ways. This, of course, has been a fact at Lincoln Electric.

Some Additional Ideas About Participation

A supervisor who has thought critically about his job of supervision comes eventually to realize that what his group of people can accomplish depends upon the degree to which each of them is genuinely interested in the work. This interest may have developed initially for all sorts of reasons, but it increases substantially in proportion to the opportunity people have to take part in planning their own work and in deciding how to do it.

Douglas McGregor, professor of management at the Massachusetts Institute of Technology, put it this way:

. . . one theme . . . recurs with remarkable frequency in reports of social science research on human relations, and of the experi-

1. James F. Lincoln, *A New Approach to Industrial Economics* (New York: The Devin-Adair Company, 1961). A readable and interesting work, despite its somewhat ponderous title.

mentation of the management pioneers. Its significance . . . depends upon whether it is imbedded in a philosophy of management or regarded as merely another fancy technique.

This recurrent theme is that of "participation." You will find it—with wide or limited emphasis—in McCormick's "multiple management," in Carey's "consultative supervision," in Given's "bottom-up management," in Barnard's "executive authority," and in a score of other well-known principles enunciated by management pioneers.

You will see its implications and its applications in much recent research—for example in the work of the late Kurt Lewin and his associates in the Research Center for Group Dynamics, and in the work of Rensis Likert and his Survey Research Center, of E. Wight Bakke, of Burleigh Gardiner, of Joseph Scanlon, of Alexander Leighton, of Robert Merton, of Alex Bavelas, and dozens of other social scientists and consultants in many different companies and universities. Surely an idea which is so often re-iterated must have more than casual significance.

So much for the background of research. Now for what participation can do, McGregor goes on to say:

It provides opportunities to bring into the work situation a variety of "on-the-job" satisfactions. It offers a potential path through the maze of problems connected with technical efficiency in plant layout, process, and work methods. It gives recognition to people as human beings, individually and in their group relations, and it brings dignity and meaning to their jobs. It can tap the creative imagination and inventive ingenuity for which we Americans are justly famous. It can banish fear and dependence by giving the members of the organization an opportunity to exert control over their own destinies and to acquire genuine understanding of what are usually felt to be mysterious and arbitrary management actions. It offers, *par excellence,* a way to encourage the development of genuine personal responsibility among all members of the organization, and with it the freedom which is always lacking when control is centralized. . . . It is, incidentally, the principle which underlies our democratic society.[2]

2. Douglas M. McGregor, "Changing Patterns in Human Relations," *Management Record,* September 1950, pp. 322–323 and 366–368.

Ideas of this kind lead to the conclusion that a supervisor is not there just to "whip up the horses," so to speak, and make them work as hard as they can. Rather, his job is to get the willing, zestful cooperation of his people in accomplishing a job which they have had a hand in planning, and which they want to do because they see it as *their* work, *their* opportunity, and *their* responsibility. The will to do must come from *within* the people, not from outside.

How then does a supervisor go about getting this willing, cooperative, zestful effort from his people? He gets it by such means as these:

1. He keeps his people fully and currently informed of everything he learns that in any way affects the work they are doing or plan to do. This is an echo of our second principle of supervision—that people must have guidance in doing their work. The supervisor, being designated by grade, salary, title, and authority as a leader of his group, is in a position to know first, ahead of his people, what his organization plans to do, what changes may be contemplated, and what effect any such changes may have on his unit. It is to him that orders come, written or oral, to take actions. In order to keep his people with him, it behooves him to see that information of this kind is passed on to his people promptly.

2. He seeks the advice and counsel of his people in the development of decisions that will affect the work they are doing. In seeking this counsel, he is bound to consider it seriously and sincerely. It may well be that he cannot take their recommendations in every instance. When he cannot, or when he can take them only in part, he must explain clearly why he cannot. His people will usually recognize that since he is held responsible for the results of the decisions, it is he who must make them. They will respect his decisions when they understand, even though they may not necessarily agree with them. It is easier for people to do this *if* they have had their full say, and *if* they understand why. Otherwise,

following a leader is pretty much a matter of blind loyalty.

3. He works with his people in attempting to solve problems facing the unit. If his people come to see these problems as *their* problems, and furthermore, if they have an active part in solving them, then the solutions are also *theirs*. It may often happen that the supervisor knows, or believes he knows, exactly what the solution ought to be. Nevertheless, it is wiser for him first to explain the problem clearly, then participate with his people in its solution. Repeatedly, experienced supervisors will tell you (no less than the social scientists) that while there are often many possible solutions, the one that the group of people can agree on is the one most likely to succeed. This, of course, is because it is the people who must try to make the solution work.

There is a pitfall to be avoided here. The supervisor who regularly tries to get his people merely to approve his own solution is in for trouble. This is not participation; it is manipulation; and few people enjoy the feeling of having been used.

4. He shares with his people the setting of goals or objectives and the performance standards for reaching them. The establishment of objectives is most commonly a job for the whole group. The setting of performance standards is necessarily individual in character, although shared by the supervisor and each person. Even here, however, the group as a whole may contribute, since how each individual may perform is related to how other individuals should perform also.

We can summarize these four points in a single idea: full participation of people in the planning and conduct of their work makes it possible for them to apply their whole intelligence to the task. This is a different thing from doing only what someone else, i.e., their supervisor, tells them to do. The idea is well summarized by E. Wight Bakke, former director of the Yale University Labor and Management Center, who notes that

it is no bed of roses and certainly no panacea for human relations problems between management and the managed. There are testimonies from managerial experience as to both successes and failures. But much evidence from psychological and social science research as well as from many outstanding practical experiments indicates that such a practice is based on a sound principle derived from the nature of human beings and their management in the doing of productive work.

The principle I have in mind is that self-realization in our culture is intimately bound up with the degree to which people are able to participate, under intelligent and rational leadership, and the degree to which they have an effective voice, in determining the rules and conditions under which, and the plans according to which, they live and work.[3]

This is a long sentence to be sure, but it is worth reading many times.

At this point, the reader will do well to turn to page 85 and to review the material headed "System 4." This is a brief description of what participation can mean in an organization, as studied at the University of Michigan by Rensis Likert.

Some Problems in Participation

There are a number of reasons that can be and have been advanced to show why participation will not or cannot work. These we need to review because, as Bakke says, there have indeed been both successes and failures with the idea. Here are some of them:

1. If we let the workers have as much to say as is implied in the idea of participation, we will have anarchy. And this we would have of course, *if* (a) there were no agreement, to start with, on what the organization was established to do, and (b) if there were no "intelligent and rational leadership" exerted. But given these two conditions, the principle of participation has been wonderfully successful in too many

3. E. Wight Bakke, "The Function of Management," in *Human Relations and Modern Management,* ed. E. M. Hugh-Jones (Amsterdam, Holland: North-Holland Publishing Company, 1958), pp. 241–242.

situations to warrant discarding it. Anarchy does not result; instead, productivity frequently booms, just as it did with the girls at Western Electric.

2. The setting of goals, planning, coordination, decision making, and control are functions that can only be correctly and properly exercised by "top management," that is, by the supervisors occupying the higher positions in the organization.

Let us consider, however, who it is that finally makes decisions effective, carries out plans, and coordinates efforts. Is it the "big boss"? Is it the supervisor of a unit? Or is it the people who are doing the work? The boss may "plan" on turning out certain work by a January 1 deadline; but the people turn out the work, and it is they who meet the deadline, *if it is met*. The executive may think he is "coordinating," but if he is successful, it is because the people are willing to work together. Any executive of experience can tell you that plans have a habit of going wrong when the people who must carry them out simply do not have their hearts in the job.

3. If we let the workers participate in planning, making important decisions, and the like, the supervisor will lose prestige and his authority will deteriorate. But the reverse has proved true in actual practice. People have respect for and enjoy working with a leader who seeks their advice and who gives it careful consideration. They can and do respect a man who works effectively *with* them. And when a man gains the respect of his people, how can it be said that he has lost prestige? The fact is, as John Cowper Powys noted long ago in his *Meaning of Culture*, that in throwing away one's soul, one frequently saves it. And with respect to authority it may be questioned whether the conventional authority is really necessary. A skillful supervisor is able to get his people to establish a goal and work hard to reach it. He need not *command* them, but only make it possible for them to exert their intelligence to set and reach such a goal.

4. Participation is another one of those management fads

that will have its day in the sun, then disappear into the limbo of forgotten notions. But the idea has been too widely and successfully practiced; it has persisted too long; and it has repeatedly been reinforced by research in many fields, often unexpectedly. It is an idea on which our system of government is based, and there has not yet appeared anywhere in the world a better idea. It is an idea firmly fixed in many of the world's greatest religions, and therefore it may be said to have important ethical roots. Far from being a fad, the idea of participation may, as McGregor says, "offer a potential path" through a maze of problems in the field of management.

It would be well for any supervisor to accord careful study to the meaning and uses of the participation idea. It is possible to experiment with it; for example, in Chapter 11 there is a discussion of methods to use in improving operating efficiency. The most fruitful of these relies heavily on participation. It has been successfully used in industrial, business, and government organizations even without the supervisory and organizational changes that ought to accompany it for fullest effectiveness. A radical change from existing supervisory practice may not be necessary; step-by-step change is apparently possible. Even so, complete changeover to participative operation is likely to produce even greater results.

One last word of caution is necessary. This is aimed especially at those organizations where participation is little used, if at all, and where the only thing the workers have to do is what they are told. The caution is this: Supervisors using participation as a regular basis for their supervisory practice feel that it requires more skill and intelligence than supervisory practice based on the old boss-subordinate idea. Experienced supervisors who have tried to change have told me that it was harder work than what they had been doing under their old system. Many of them added, however, that it was not only more effective, once they got it going, but that after a while ("when you get used to it") it became easy.

As Robert K. Burns pointed out in the April 1959 issue

of *Public Personnel Review,* "the art of leadership, in the words of a great general, consists in getting people to do what you want done because they want to do it."

6   *Something About Motivation*

In 1959 Frederick Herzberg and his associates in Pittsburgh published a report on their research entitled *The Motivation to Work*.[1] These psychologists had been trying to get a convincing answer to the question: What do people want from their jobs? They wanted to find out what factors affect a worker's attitude or feelings toward his job. They also wanted to know whether these feelings made any difference in the way people work, that is, in how productive they are.

Of course, many other scientists had worked on this problem, and the Pittsburgh investigators reviewed everything they could find that had been done before.[2] In general, they were not satisfied that the published information could answer these questions conclusively. But in reviewing the literature they did find one possibly important idea. They noticed that when investigators asked people what they *liked* about their jobs, they got one kind of answer; when they asked people what they *did not like* about their jobs, they got another kind of answer. It seemed from this that there might be a difference between the factors that had to do with good feelings about a job and the factors that had to do with bad feelings.

So the Pittsburgh investigators started to study people's attitudes about their jobs with such an idea in mind. They made their study in nine companies in and around Pittsburgh, and they aimed it at engineers and accountants, a hundred of each. They used a very simple approach. "Think of a time," they asked each man, "when you felt exceptionally good about your job—either the one you have now or any

1. Frederick Herzberg, Bernard Mausner, and B. B. Snyderman, *The Motivation to Work* (New York: John Wiley & Sons, 1959).

2. The results of this review work were also published: Frederick Herzberg, *et al., Job Attitudes: Review of Research and Opinion* (Psychological Services of Pittsburgh, 1957).

other job you have had. Tell us what happened." They checked the man's story very carefully. When did this happen? How long did you feel good? Why did this make you feel good? How long did you feel this way? How did this affect the way you did your job? These and many more questions were aimed at getting as clear and specific answers as possible. As soon as one story was completed, the investigators asked for another, this time one of when a man felt very bad about something that happened on his job. And again, a series of questions seeking clear and specific answers.

All told, the investigators obtained about 476 such stories from the 200 engineers and accountants. Next they analyzed critically what they had found. This is a well-known technique—the interview and then analysis of the answers—that is regularly used by psychologists and by analysts of public opinion polls. In their report, the investigators recorded exactly how they analyzed the information, how they coded it, how they checked the accuracy of their coding, and so on. This account is of great interest to other scientists, but we can simply note here that the job was well and carefully done. The results are what may be of greatest interest to supervisors.

The Job-Satisfying Factors

The investigators found five factors or ideas that the people mentioned most often when they talked about feeling good about their jobs. Arranged in the order of frequency with which they were mentioned, these were:
1. Achievement.
2. Recognition.
3. The work itself.
4. Responsibility.
5. Advancement.
This is what the investigators meant by these factors:
1. *Achievement.* This factor was mentioned most often. In the stories about good feelings, some 41 percent revolved

around something the people had done that was successful. There were all kinds of stories about many kinds of jobs. In each one, though, the man felt that he had done something in which he could take pride. He was satisfied and pleased with his achievement.

2. *Recognition.* Here the people told how someone recognized their good work and complimented them in some way about it. They got a pat on the back from a customer, or the boss, or an associate, or a subordinate. Usually the recognition was associated with achievement.

3. *The work itself.* This factor involved work that was interesting, challenging, varied, or that could be carried through from beginning to end. The engineers and accountants got great satisfaction out of working at creative tasks, whether recognition came or not.

4. *Responsibility.* Under this factor, people talked about jobs they did without supervision, for which they were fully responsible. Sometimes this was responsibility for a new kind of work, without advancement; sometimes it was responsibility for the work of other people.

5. *Advancement.* This means the employee was promoted. In half the stories, the promotion was a surprise; the man had not expected it. This factor usually involved increases in pay, but in the study it was separated from salary, as a factor in itself.

Good feelings that came to the people for these five reasons tended to last a long time after the events involved. Interestingly, the good feelings about responsibility, the work itself, and advancement lasted longest of all. This trio is much more potent, so to speak, than achievement or recognition insofar as their lasting effects are concerned. On the other hand, achievement and recognition head the list of factors that are most frequently associated with people's satisfaction about their jobs. In any event, it turned out that these factors were closely associated with each other, and that they were responsible in largest part for feelings of satisfaction that the workers had about their jobs.

The Job-Dissatisfying Factors

Next the Pittsburgh investigators turned to the factors that were mentioned most often by the men as they told about instances when they were unhappy about their jobs. As the investigators had expected, the factors leading to job dissatisfaction were not the same as the factors just discussed. Instead, different factors appeared in most of the accounts. These were:

1. Company policy and administration.
2. Technical supervision.
3. Salary.
4. Interpersonal supervision.
5. Working conditions.

Again, we list these and explain what the investigators meant by them:

1. *Company policy and administration.* This had to do with company inefficiency, waste, duplication of effort, or a struggle for power. But more of the stories that mentioned this factor had to do with personnel and other policies that were unfair or positively harmful to the people. Frequently, salary was mentioned along with policy and administration.

2. *Technical supervision.* This factor had nothing to do with social relations between the men and their supervisors (see factor 4, below, for this) but with lack of competence on the part of the supervisor. Supervisors were mentioned who simply did not know how to supervise the technical work for which they were responsible, or who were unfair.

3. *Salary.* This factor was mentioned in both the good stories and the bad. However, in the stories of unhappy feelings, salary was mentioned as part of an unfair system of wage administration. In the stories of good feelings, salary was simply part of advancement, hence good. The scientists

concluded that unfair handling of salaries—wage increases given too late or reluctantly, or too little difference between the salaries of new and older employees—was, therefore, a factor of most importance in leading to dissatisfaction.

4. *Interpersonal supervision.* This factor refers to the personal relationships between the workers and their supervisor. When the men could not "get along" with their boss, they felt bad about their jobs. Frequently this factor was closely associated with factor 2, poor technical supervision.

5. *Working conditions.* This had to do with poor facilities, inconvenient location of the plant, and the amount of work the men had to do on the job. It is to the credit of the men interviewed that they complained of not enough work, rather than too much.

The workers' unhappy feelings about their jobs came largely as a result of the operation of these five factors. There were two additional feelings the workers mentioned very frequently as a result. They felt that the company was unfair. And they felt that they were not getting anywhere in their jobs. The stories they told, in which they mentioned one or more of the five factors, were of events that made them feel that they were being treated unfairly and that prospects for professional growth looked pretty grim.

Parenthetically, we may note here that expert supervision can throw the five satisfying factors into full operation—at least as supervision is defined and used in this book. In the study we are discussing here, supervision, both technical and interpersonal, has a special meaning given to it by the investigators. It would be well not to confuse the two meanings.

Some Conclusions About the Factors

The findings talked about so far lead to the following general conclusions:

1. There are five factors of importance that lead people to be satisfied and happy with their jobs. These are achieve-

ment, recognition, the challenge of the work itself, responsibility, and advancement. These factors revolve around the idea that people want to grow and develop professionally in their work. They want to develop themselves to their fullest capacity as creative and unique individuals. This is the concept of self-realization or fulfillment that many psychologists have noted as having a profound effect on what people do to achieve their ultimate goal in life. The Pittsburgh study indicates that when people can realize their hopes and ambitions in the work they do, they like their work, derive pleasure from it, and enjoy a high level of satisfaction with their jobs.

2. There is a group of five other significant factors that operate in the opposite direction, that is, that lead people to be unhappy and dissatisfied with their jobs. These are unfair or unsatisfactory administrative practice, supervision, compensation, and working conditions. These factors have little to do with personal growth of individuals. Instead, they are associated with the conditions that surround the doing of the job. They act to make the job environment unsatisfactory to people, and hence they bring about feelings of dissatisfaction.

3. The two groups of factors—the "satisfiers" and the "dissatisfiers"—operate more or less independently of each other and in different directions. The satisfying factors lead people to feel good about their work. The other factors lead in the opposite direction, that is, to dissatisfaction with the job.

This was a new idea at the time. Until this study was made, the generally accepted notion was that any factor that affected people operated in a straight line. Thus, if poor working conditions caused people to become dissatisfied with their jobs, the presumption was that improved working conditions would cause people to become satisfied. But the study does not show this to be true. All one can say is that if working conditions are improved, people's dissatisfactions may disappear, but we still do not get much in the way of satisfaction with the job. Likewise, if the satisfying factors of achievement and recognition operate to make people feel good about their work, the lack of these factors does not (i.e., did not) lead to dissatisfaction. We can summarize this by saying that satisfying factors affect job attitudes mostly in a positive way, while dissatisfying factors affect job attitudes mostly in a negative way.

Performance Effects

We may recall that one of the questions the interviewers asked was, "How did this incident (good or bad) affect the way you did your job?" This information they got from the men was not put in terms of exactly how much more or less they produced. Rather, what they got was an account of the effect on their performance—whether they worked harder and produced more, or whether they quit trying and produced less. In a nutshell, the results, then, were:

1. In about three out of four of the accounts in which the men felt good about their job, an improvement in performance was stated as a result of their better feelings about the work. The investigators list some of the statements made, indicating that the men started working harder, more effectively, longer hours, with greater enthusiasm, doing part of the work at home, and so on. Furthermore, many of these effects lasted for a long time.

2. In about half of the accounts in which the men felt unhappy about their jobs, a decline in work performance took place as a result. The men said they put off doing things, did not care whether the work got out or not, were not able to work as they had before, quit trying, slowed down, and so on. Here also, many of these performance effects lasted a long time.

There were various other effects. In about half the stories about unsatisfactory events, the men told of thinking about quitting, or of taking steps to quit; some actually did quit. Clear evidence appeared that loyalty to the company, or or-

ganization, varied with the degree of job satisfaction. When
the men felt good about their work, they felt better about the
company, and vice versa.

It is worth charting these effects:

I Satisfiers lead to:	II Dissatisfiers lead to:
Increased interest	Decreased interest
Increased enthusiasm	Decreased enthusiasm
Increased productivity	Decreased productivity
	An *increase* in quits

This chart summarizes results that are of considerable importance to supervisors. The increases in group I are almost
exactly what any supervisor hopes for and tries to get in his
unit. The decreases—and the increase in quits—in group II
are the things he hopes to avoid. Here is a direct relationship
between motivation and performance effects. If a supervisor
could set the "satisfier" factors into operation, he might expect
the results in group I. If he could block or nullify the operation of the "dissatisfiers" he might expect fewer or none of
the results in group II. These are exciting prospects.

Finally, our investigators found no differences in the effects
reported either by accountants or engineers, or in different
age groups, or job levels. In other words, attitudes about work
are probably true of people in general, regardless of their
age, salary, or the kind of work they do.

The investigators noted that there have been many contradictory reports with respect to the relation between morale
and productivity. They suspect this may be so because previous studies may have confused the factors found in the good
and bad sequences of this particular study.

Later Studies

A whole series of studies followed the one made by Herzberg
and his associates. One after another these investigations con-

firmed the findings of the original Pittsburgh investigation. The evidence, indeed, is now overwhelming that the Motivator-Hygiene theory[3] is essentially correct.

The original study included only two hundred workers, which was a small sample on which to base a theory about people in general. By this time, however, more than twenty thousand people have been involved in similar studies. Included within this number were people working at more than sixty distinctly different kinds of jobs. Some fifty studies were made by a number of psychologists and physicians, some of whom used Herzberg's methods and some of whom used other approaches. This last point has significance, indicating as it does that the results were not necessarily associated with methodology.

The later studies included a sizable number of women as well as men. They dealt with skilled and unskilled workers as well as professionals. One study included more than one hundred Negro workers. And some included Scandinavian and Hungarian workers; these were conducted by Herzberg himself. His more recent efforts were aimed at workers in the Soviet Union, and first indications were that results would be the same there as in the United States, Scandinavia, and Hungary.

It is worthwhile listing at least some of the many kinds of workers studied. They included:

Scientists (chemists, physicists, mathematicians, and others).

Supervisors (foremen in a number of industries, managers).

Engineers (general, chemical, ordnance, aeronautical).

Accountants.

Extension agents.

Unskilled workers (food, engineering, and maintenance services).

---

3. The theory is often referred to in this way. The "satisfier" factors were called motivators. The "dissatisfiers" were called hygiene factors in a sort of parallel to medical hygiene, meaning preventive medicine and having to do with keeping an environment healthful.

Nurses.

Women executives.

Air Force officers.

Nonsupervisory personnel (in a variety of firms and government agencies).

College students.

Automobile assembly-line workers.

Women assembly-line workers.

In some of the studies, findings also showed that the theory applied to people regardless of their age, sex, salaries, educational background, personality characteristics, and of course, the kind of work they were doing. This was additional confirmation of the original study.

All this leads to the conclusion that a supervisor can rely on the Motivator-Hygiene theory with confidence.[4]

Putting the Study Results to Use

The conclusions of the Pittsburgh and later studies coincide remarkably well with experience. Supervisors readily agree that no matter how fairly people are treated, and no matter how pleasant their working conditions, they do not really do their best until they have the freedom to show what they are capable of doing. And this in turn takes challenging tasks, full responsibility, and recognition of successful work, not only by a pat on the back, but by actual promotion.

As we have already noted, the concept of supervision in the study appeared to be somewhat restrictive. As we use the term in this book, supervision includes everything a supervisor can do to bring about the greatest possible combined effectiveness of his people in getting work done. Thus a supervisor needs to consider not only how he can eliminate job dissatisfaction, but also, and perhaps more importantly, how he

4. Many of the later investigations discussed here are portrayed in detail in *Work and the Nature of Man,* by Frederick Herzberg (Cleveland and New York: The World Publishing Company, 1966).

can bring about job satisfaction. He must see what he can do about both kinds of factors, those that produce negative effects and those that produce positive ones.

In the material that follows, we consider the ways in which supervisors can make it possible for the factors of the Pittsburgh study to operate to best advantage. There are some over which the supervisor has almost full control, some that will come into play according to the initiative of the supervisor, and some over which he can exert little or no control. As we review these matters, we must note that there are tremendous variations in the policies and administration of different organizations, whether industrial or business concerns, and also among government agencies.

The Satisfiers

Several general points need to be made at the outset. The Pittsburgh investigators noted that the factors operating in a negative direction—the "dissatisfiers"—form a sort of base on top of which the "satisfiers" can operate. This implies that until job dissatisfaction is eliminated, one can scarcely expect the satisfying factors to exert their fullest effect. Perhaps this is so, but possibly only to a limited extent. All experienced supervisors are aware that the challenge and stimulation of the work itself, plus responsibility, achievement, and recognition, can often outweigh low salaries, unsatisfactory policies, and poor working conditions. Many teachers teach because they love to work; they will tolerate a great deal in order to keep on teaching. Similarly, many people in the government service, or in church organizations, or in business, or in industry are there because they believe in the work they are doing—despite handicapping factors of one kind or another.

A second general point is that supervisors usually have it within their power to put most or all of the "satisfier" factors into full operation. This is in contrast to the negative "dissatisfiers," over which the supervisor can ordinarily exert much less direct control. It should be obvious that no supervisor can press a button and cause his workers to jump in response. What *is* possible, however, is for almost any supervisor to arrange things so that (1) the "satisfier" factors can operate, and (2) the "dissatisfiers" are minimized.

We review the "satisfiers," then, in a slightly different order than they appear in the study. We do this merely to make our points easier to review. For each factor we consider the question: What specific things can a supervisor do to make it possible for the factor to motivate his people as fully as possible?

1. THE WORK ITSELF

Three important possibilities seem obvious with respect to this factor. The first is that a supervisor needs to make a real and convincing effort to be sure his people understand the importance of the work they do. Their job—whatever it is—relates in one way or another to the larger purpose of the organization. In turn, this larger purpose may relate to the welfare of the community, to the service of the public, or an important segment of the public, to the good of the nation itself, or, indeed, to the benefit of humanity—all this depending on the organization. Thus jobs can be shown to be closely and directly related to this broader purpose. It is true that many may not seem to be, and that routine, simple tasks may seem indirectly related indeed; but it is not so much a matter of the immediate job as it is the effect of that job on the broader purpose. The supervisor should not make this sort of thing ridiculous. No use trying to fool people into thinking they are important when they are not. But there is a legitimate bit of salesmanship here that a supervisor needs to think about. He is well advised to reread the short section on Principle One in Chapter 2; it bears on this point.

The second specific thing a supervisor can do is rearrange the work performed by his unit, so that each job is made as interesting as possible to each person concerned. So much depends on the nature of the work that it is hard to be specific here. However, in order to arrange things so that people will find the greatest possible satisfaction with their work—and thereby become more productive—we must go to some lengths to avoid the boring, the repetitive, the monotonous tasks that conspire to make work uninteresting and even downright unpleasant. Industry is facing this kind of a question; there is doubt about the productivity of people on the production line compared to their productivity in restructured, challenging jobs.[5]

Third is the question of whether a man is placed in the best job *for him.* Personnel people talk about this as "placement." If the placement is poor, the man may fail to find the job interesting and challenging. The question—to both the man and his supervisor—is whether the man might be more effective and productive in another kind of job than the one he finds lacking in challenge. We will assume here that the two points above have been tried, but that restructuring the job or explaining its broader purpose has no effect. Then a supervisor had better help the man look around him for work in which he can find an interest. Doing this raises problems, to be sure. But too many people manage, somehow, to work out their whole lives at jobs they really do not believe in, do not care about, and would leave if they only could see their way clear.

2. RESPONSIBILITY

Letting this motivating factor operate is well within the power of nearly all supervisors. There are three concrete possibilities.

The first, and for many supervisors the most difficult one, is to refrain from supervising too closely. Oversupervision tends to stifle initiative. Let the man work! Give him the

5. Industrial and government supervisors alike will find it worthwhile to read Douglas M. McGregor, *The Human Side of Enterprise* (New York: McGraw-Hill Book Co., 1960).

freedom he must have if he is to show what he can do. By such means, people's sense of responsibility for their work can be sharpened.

The second thing a supervisor can do is to assign a man more responsible tasks to perform. With this assignment, the supervisor again refrains from watching his man too closely. The man has to be put "on his own" insofar as the work permits. Here the supervisor is trying to build the sense of responsibility each of his people should have.

The third specific thing a supervisor can do to develop more responsible people is to utilize the principle of participation discussed in the latter part of Chapter 5. As people come to share in solving the unit's problems and in helping make decisions, their sense of responsibility deepens. This has been proved beyond question by supervisors experienced in using the participative approach in the work of their units. It amounts to a sharing of responsibility for what is done.

3. ACHIEVEMENT

This factor is next because it is more likely to become completely effective after the two factors above are in full operation. With full responsibility for an interesting job, a man can be expected to try to bring it off successfully. The opportunity to achieve has to be carefully created. With this in mind, a supervisor can do such specific things as these:

First, he must study the work and his people with a view to providing opportunities in which they can attempt to achieve results. If at all possible, these opportunities should be such as to make his people extend themselves. They must have a chance at a task as creative in character as possible. If they can meet the challenge, the pride of achievement they experience will be for something more than the ordinary.

Next, the supervisor must encourage his people to attempt doing something they may not quite believe they can do. By every appropriate means at his command he must urge and lead them on. He should be careful to avoid "whipping up the horses"; what he wants is to get people to see that they have the opportunity, have the responsibility, and have the ability to tackle the task.

Finally, the supervisor must get the recognition factor to work as quickly as he sees his people successful in performing a difficult or challenging piece of work. Achievement without recognition is somewhat like apple pie without cheese. The pie is good in itself, but the cheese helps make it just a little bit better.

4. RECOGNITION

The operation of this factor, as we have just noted, is very closely related to achievement. In fact, it is seldom dissociated. Whatever people achieve—either a specific thing or a long-continued and sustained effort—recognition ought to be prompt and clear. Nothing in any rule or regulation of any government agency or industrial concern prevents a supervisor from recognizing the good work of his people. In fact, of all the responsibilities a supervisor has, this one is more easily exercised than any other. It is indeed a cardinal principle of supervision, as we noted in Chapter 2. Specific ways in which a supervisor can give recognition are listed under Principle Three in that chapter. All of them depend, however, on the premise that he first learn to recognize achievement on the part of his people when it occurs.

5. ADVANCEMENT

Here we have the only motivating factor among the "satisfiers" over which the supervisor may not be able to exert full control. On the other hand, he can have about as much to do with its operation as anyone else, and ordinarily it is he who must set it in motion. His specific actions leading to activation of this factor should be these:

To start with, he will need to train his people for more

responsible work. (This idea is discussed under Principle Five in Chapter 2, and in Chapter 8; on training.) The supervisor will also need to do all he can at this point to encourage his people to improve themselves. All of this is aimed, of course, at preparing his people for advancement. The training he does and the way in which his people discharge greater responsibilities must, of necessity, be put in the record, that is, in the personnel folder. This is part of the preparation for advancement.

Second, a supervisor recommends the people in his group who are well prepared and ready for advancement. If those he recommends make good, his recommendations will gradually gain weight. If they do not, or if only a few do, his later recommendations will lose weight. The supervisor simply must make sure that his recommended people can make the grade. This means, of course, that he must assure himself all along that his records of accepted and discharged responsibilities are well founded.

We might add, by way of summary, that if a supervisor can set these five motivating factors into full operation, he has a better than average chance of developing a group of employees who find great satisfaction in their work. It is likely that these factors may outweigh the dissatisfiers, which we discuss in the following section.

The Dissatisfiers

In this group of five factors leading to job dissatisfaction, two are fully within the control of supervisors. These are the two kinds of "supervision" outlined by the Pittsburgh study—technical and interpersonal. This entire book is concerned with the many ways in which a supervisor can improve his supervision. There would be little point in repeating them here, except to note that supervising is itself a job to which one has to apply the greatest possible intelligence.

It is a thinking, planning, studying, analyzing kind of work. It is as challenging as any other kind of work we have. The man who does not understand or believe this should, without doubt, get into some other kind of work that will give him greater personal satisfaction.

There are a number of complicating problems associated with the activation of the other three factors, at least insofar as supervisors are concerned. These—policy, salary, and working conditions—most supervisors do not control, except in small part. Their efforts with respect to these factors must of necessity have to do with influencing others to help bring them into full operation.

1. POLICY AND ADMINISTRATION

The Pittsburgh study mentioned personnel policy in particular. This policy is rarely or never set by individual supervisors. Rather, it is stated by or emanates from the board of directors plus the managing heads of a company; in the federal service, it is set government-wide by the actions of Congress, the President, and the Civil Service Commission. In both industry and the government, personnel policy is importantly influenced in one way or another by the action of unions. Sometimes the policies may be stated in writing; sometimes they may be no more than a body of unwritten principles based largely on precedent. But no personnel policy, written or unwritten, is any better than the administration thereof. If any policy is successful, it is because supervisors make it so. The policy is in their hands to make of it what they can or will.

Of key importance with respect to personnel policy is the need for a career system in any organization. Some businesses and industries have excellent systems, and some may have none at all. In the federal government, some agencies or bureaus likewise have excellent systems, and again, some have none at all. Political scientists have pointed this out before,[6] noting that true career systems and policies occur more or less as islands in the federal service. A supervisor in one of these—just as in the outstanding industrial organizations—is fortunate; he may operate accordingly. The supervisor not on one of these islands can only try to reach shore by continually urging his organization to develop—and really implement—all aspects of a true career system.

Thus, while individual supervisors are in no position to set personnel policy, they can undertake to be as fair and enlightened in their supervisory practice as it is possible to be. Within whatever organizational climate they may enjoy, they can develop a small climate of their own, in their own units, in which it may be possible to eliminate a large part of the dissatisfaction that might otherwise occur.

2. SALARY

With respect to this factor, as well as the one above, the supervisor can do relatively little except to see that government-wide or company-wide policy is carried out as well as possible. Pay scales are rarely set these days by any individual supervisor. He may, of course, act with a union to foster the best possible wage and salary administration. But this is not action as a supervisor; it is action of a union member.

As between government and industry, salaries and wages tend always toward a balance. If at one time government salaries lag behind those of industry, at other times they exceed them. If there is a sizable discrepancy between salaries of similar positions in government and industry, a series of factors operate gradually to equalize them. At any given time, great capital may be made of observable differences, but given time, such differences are quite likely to disappear.

In any event, in either industry or government the super-

6. The interested reader will find a very full discussion of this in the *Federal Government Service: Its Character, Prestige, and Problems*. Report of the American Assembly (New York: Columbia University Graduate School of Business, 1955).

visor has the opportunity, indeed the responsibility, for seeing that positions under his control are properly compensated for the work performed in them—under whatever system they may operate. In the government service this means that he must understand how jobs are classified, what classification standards and specifications are, and something about how they are applied. He need not become a classification analyst himself, but he should be able to discuss classification problems intelligently with such analysts. This is not to say that he should simply be adept at arguments or that he should be skilled at "blowing up" job elements. Rather, on the basis of his knowledge of classification, he should be in a position to recognize new or additional elements that may affect the grade of his job. And he should call prompt attention to these changes. If he does not get the grade he hoped for, he should make it his business to see that his people understand why. His explanation should, in all fairness, omit reference to the so-and-so who classified the work.

3. WORKING CONDITIONS

Most supervisors are in a sort of halfway position with respect to this factor. They can do a great deal to make working conditions reasonable. But there may be some working conditions they can do little or nothing about. Organizational units tightly packed in their offices for lack of space may wait a long time for the new building. Air-conditioning may be hard to get. Lighting may sometimes be slow in coming. Location of the office may not always suit most employees, and transportation may be horrible, as it is in many of our big cities.

On the other hand, within the facilities available a supervisor can do quite a little. He can generate a friendly and businesslike atmosphere. He can make the most of the office furniture. He can watch the safety and health hazards and reduce them. He can enlist the participation of his people in solving problems with respect to working conditions in ways on which they all can agree. And then he can continue to press for improvements. The knowledge that the boss is trying often helps to make poor conditions tolerable.

Some Concluding Thoughts

This chapter is different from most of the other chapters in this book since it is based entirely on the results of scientific studies. Also, it goes into greater detail. I wanted it to be an example of what we might have in every aspect of supervisory work if we had sufficient scientific research on which to base the most enlightened supervision possible.

From the standpoint of practical application, the reader should understand that there has already been widespread application of the Herzberg theory in both industry and government. It has been used as a basis for personnel programs, training programs, management development, and recruitment. It has been used in morale surveys, quality control, wage and salary administration, and job enlargement. Supervisors in both government and industry have been shown how to use it, and "top management" groups have used it to nullify the operation of the "dissatisfier" factors. The skillful application of this theory to management has been generally successful.[7]

For reasons such as these, as well as those already discussed, supervisors everywhere will do well to consider how they might apply these ideas to their own particular situations.

---

7. A full discussion of the remarkable results achieved at Bell Telephone is to be found in *Motivation Through the Work Itself* by Robert N. Ford, (New York: American Management Association, 1969). See also M. Scott Myers, "Who Are Your Motivated Workers?", *Harvard Business Review*, January–February 1964, pp. 73–88, for an account of the use of the Herzberg theory at Texas Instruments.

7   New Insights into Human Behavior

For a number of years behavioral scientists have been studying the factors that motivate people. Maslow,[1] for example, developed the interesting and useful concept that the needs of human beings are organized in a series of levels. At the very bottom are needs for sheer physical survival—for oxygen, food, water, sleep, shelter. Next above them are safety needs —for protection against threat or danger. Above these are social needs—for belonging, for friendship, association, love. And on the top level are the egoistic needs—for self-confidence, achievement, knowledge, and for status, recognition, and the appreciation and respect of others.

Maslow's idea is that the physical needs of a human being must first be satisfied before he can think about much else. Man devotes all the attention required to getting enough to eat, to drink, or to protecting himself from the elements. Once these needs are satisfied and he is no longer hungry, or cold, or thirsty, his behavior begins to be motivated by his needs for safety. When he was hungry he may have got food under conditions of extreme hazard. But with plenty of food, he thinks twice before risking danger. He is now motivated importantly by his need for protection from it.

Generally speaking, once the lower-level needs are met, the higher levels become increasingly important as motivators of behavior. Thus it is that in our relatively affluent society, supervisors find their people motivated most commonly by egoistic needs—at the top level—and to a lesser extent by the social needs. Physical and safety needs are pretty well taken care of.

Now note that the egoistic needs are essentially the same as the "satisfier" factors developed by Frederick Herzberg. It could be said that the Herzberg and related studies have

1. A. H. Maslow, *Motivation and Personality* (New York: Harper & Row, 1954).

provided strong support for Maslow's theory, certainly insofar as the top-level, egoistic needs are concerned.

Theory X and Theory Y

A few years before Herzberg's study first appeared, Douglas
McGregor published his now famous theory X and theory
Y.[2] His ideas correlate well with the findings of Herzberg
and with Maslow's theory.

McGregor pointed out that there are two contrasting points
of view about how to manage human beings in an organization. The usual point of view embodies such ideas as these:

1. Most human beings dislike work and will avoid it if
they can.

2. They have little or no ambition, dislike responsibility,
and prefer to be led.

3. They are self-centered and are indifferent to the needs
of the organization.

4. They resist change and want security above all.

5. They are not very bright, and they are easily misled by
demagogues.

These beliefs about human beings are widespread, Mc-
Gregor thought. They form the basis for management in
many organizations. They influence managerial action in a
major way. It is management's responsibility to organize and
operate the enterprise. To do this it uses money, materials,
equipment, and people to produce goods or services. This
must be done efficiently if the enterprise is to be successful.
In order to get people to work as well and hard as possible,
management has to take a strong hand. It must direct people's
activities, persuade them, reward them, punish them, control
them. All this has to be done in order to get people to do
what the organization wants.

2. Douglas M. McGregor, "The Human Side of Enterprise," in *Proceedings
Fifth Anniversary Convocation of the School of Industrial Management, Massachusetts Institute of Technology,* Cambridge, 1957. Also under the same title,
in book form (New York: McGraw-Hill Book Co., 1960).

This whole set of beliefs and assumptions, and the style of management based on them, McGregor has called theory X. But, as he said, this theory of management by direction and control is failing in our present-day society. It does not provide for the effective motivation of people whose physical and safety needs are satisfied, and whose social and egoistic needs are therefore dominant.

Obviously, we need a better understanding of human nature than is to be found in the theory X assumptions. McGregor used the findings of many behavioral scientists, including Maslow. Later he pointed to Herzberg's motivational theory as supporting a whole new set of assumptions about human behavior. This new set he called theory Y.

Theory Y consists of a series of ideas or assumptions that are strongly supported by the findings of scientists in recent years. These assumptions are as follows:

1. Human beings don't necessarily dislike work. They may enjoy it, or they may not. If the work is a source of satisfaction to them, they will perform it willingly. If not, or if it is a source of punishment, then, of course, they will avoid it.

2. Direction, control, rewards, and threat of punishment are not the only means to get people to work for organizational goals. Human beings will work hard and well to achieve objectives they believe in.

3. The satisfaction of egoistic needs (for achievement, recognition, self-confidence, etc.) can come about as people work toward these objectives that they have adopted.

4. Under the right conditions, the average human being wants and will seek responsibility. (Remember the Herzberg "satisfiers.")

5. Imagination, ingenuity, and creativity are characteristics that most human beings, not just a few, possess. By and large, McGregor notes, people don't get the opportunity to display such characteristics in modern industry. When they do, the industry benefits.

What management has to do, McGregor felt, is to arrange

things so that management and the people can work together for the success of the enterprise. He called this the principle of integration. It was stated in other words by James Lincoln in 1914 when he said that if he could get all the employees to want the company to succeed as badly as he did, there ought to be no limits to what they could do together (as noted on p. 51). What he did, in fact, was run the company in such a way that the people in it could achieve their personal goals best by working for the success of the company.

As most of us know, however, the practices of the Lincoln Company have not been widely adopted. McGregor did not feel that his theory Y would be widely or readily adopted either. The trouble is, management goes on thinking in terms of theory X. And it may be a long time before management is utilizing fully and widely the ideas in theory Y. But organizational operation is moving in the direction McGregor thought it should. Where this is taking place, remarkable results are coming about. The people in the organization are being encouraged to develop and use their knowledge, skills, abilities, and imagination to help reach the objectives of the organization. They do this because the company's objectives are theirs also. And in working toward these objectives the people find deep satisfaction in their achievement.

System 4

Beginning in 1947 the Institute for Social Research at the University of Michigan began studying the human problems involved in management. Rensis Likert, director of the Institute, headed up the studies. In 1961 he published a summary of findings[3] and a new theory of management based on scientific research. More recently he has added to his original theory and supplied additional proof of its usefulness.[4]

3. Rensis Likert, *New Patterns of Management* (New York: McGraw-Hill Book Co., 1961).
4. Rensis Likert, *The Human Organization: Its Management and Value* (New York: McGraw-Hill Book Co., 1967).

Likert describes four different kinds of management systems:

System 1 he calls Exploitive-Authoritative. This system resembles closely the style of management based on the ideas and assumptions of McGregor's theory X. Threats, punishment, control, and direction are characteristic. The workers feel no responsibility for the organization's goals, do not participate in decisions. Managers don't trust their people, and the people don't trust the managers. The workers are supposed to do as they are told, and they usually find ways to resist or oppose management. Employees generally are afraid or reluctant to express their ideas about the work.

Systems 2 and 3 grade between 1 and 4. System 2 is the Benevolent-Authoritative system, a little better than system 1. System 3, the Consultive system, lies between 2 and 4. It is better than 2, but not as good as system 4.

System 4, which Likert calls the Participative system, stands in greatest contrast to system 1. It resembles closely the style of management based on the ideas and assumptions in McGregor's theory Y. Under this system people at every level feel a real responsibility for the organization's goals, and they work hard to reach them. There is real participation throughout, and the people help in making important decisions. Managers have complete confidence and trust in their people, and the people reciprocate. There is complete freedom to express ideas about the work.

In discussing the four systems, Likert points out that the theory X ideas implicit in system 1 must give way to theory Y ideas if system 4 is to become operative. There must also be much greater use of the motivational forces of self-actualization, i.e., more use of Herzberg's "satisfiers." Greater participation must be practiced. Better communication must be made possible both up and down.

The close parallel among the findings and thinking of Likert, Herzberg, Maslow, and McGregor is apparent. And there are dozens of other behaviorial scientists who, in one way or another, have come forward with findings that support the work of these four.

Likert, however, using some simple but ingenious methods, has been able to relate productivity to his systems. He uses figures for the most part from industrial concerns, but he has a few from government units also. He and his associates have now shown conclusively that the nearer the management system is to system 4, the more productive the organization is. But this is not all. System 4 management results also in lower costs and higher earnings. It results in better union relations, fewer strikes, fewer work stoppages. And it results in better worker attitudes and higher morale.

Conversely, of course, the nearer the management system is to system 1, the lower the productivity, the higher the costs, the lower the company earnings, the poorer the union relations, and the lower the morale.

Likert believes that with more scientific facts a still better system could be developed. Right now, system 4 is clearly the best we know how to achieve. But when we know more, we may have a system 5 or 6 that may help us to do even more.

There is little question that system 4 takes more knowledge and skill. It may take several months for a supervisor to learn. It also requires that the entire top management of an organization consciously and deliberately undertake to foster it. Likert believes it takes up to a year to prove to all the people that the system (1, 2, or 3) is really changing (to 4). Only when the entire organization is convinced, do the results begin to show up. Once under way and used with skill, system 4 can produce results previously impossible.

Is it possible to change a manager? The whole "top management" of an organization? Likert cites actual examples showing that it can, that, indeed, it has been done.[5]

5. A recent work by Alfred T. Marrow entitled "The Failure of Success," published by Amacom, a division of the American Management Association, New York, 1972, offers additional and important examples, well worth reviewing.

McClelland's Work

In the meantime, at Harvard other work has been going on which offers considerable promise. David McClelland, director of the Center for Research in Personality, and his associates have been studying the whole question of achievement for the past twenty years.[6]

He notes that some human beings are challenged by opportunity and feel impelled to work hard to achieve something. Most human beings, though, are apparently much less interested. McClelland thought it might be possible to develop the desire to achieve in people who apparently had very little of it.

It was found, to start with, that people with a strong need or desire to achieve exhibit such characteristics as these:

1. They set goals for themselves that they have to stretch a little to achieve. The goals are not impossibly high, nor ridiculously easy. But they are a challenge to excel.

2. They set goals like this only if they can personally influence the outcome by doing the work themselves. They don't like to gamble, because they don't like to leave the outcome to chance.

3. They enjoy the work itself and are most concerned with their personal achievement. They work not so much for the rewards of their success as for the success itself.

4. They prefer work in which they can get concrete readings on how well they are doing. They want to know their score, so to speak, as they go along.

The reason why some men act this way is that they habitually spend their time thinking about doing things better, McClelland says. It appears that they don't inherit this trait; they get it from the way their parents work with them as

---

6. David C. McClelland, "Toward a Theory of Motive Acquisition," *American Psychologist*, 20: 321–333, 1965. Also by the same author, "That Urge to Achieve," in *Think*, November–December 1966, pp. 19–23.

children. The parents set moderate goals for them, then are warm, encouraging, and nonauthoritative in helping them reach the goals.

The Harvard scientists can determine this need for achievement in people by some simple tests. People with high scores —that is, with a high need or desire for achievement—get promoted more rapidly, make more money, and in general do better than other people.

McClelland and his associates more recently have been trying to find ways of developing this need for achievement in people. They have developed a course in which such training is attempted. They have, he notes, put everything into the course that they feel may help to change people. And in a number of cases, the course has produced highly satisfactory results.

Executives from a number of companies both in America, and in India and Mexico, have taken the course. Two years after completion, careful statistical studies showed that the men who took the course had done much better than comparable groups of men who had not. The executives expanded their businesses faster, made more money, were promoted faster, displayed greater initiative in new ventures, and so on.

The Mexican executives were an exception; reviews of their activities did not show them to have developed greater need for achievement as measured. In other studies, the Harvard scientists had difficulty with students from low-income groups, although they were successful with medium-income students. They are not sure yet just why this is so, and a great deal more research may be required in order to find out. But they are working hard to develop the techniques. After all, as McClelland himself states, they have "a tremendous potential for contributing to human betterment."

Here again let us note some interesting interrelationships. Maslow classified the needs of human beings, with egoistic needs, including the need for achievement, at the top level. McGregor developed theory Y, aimed at satisfying the egoistic needs. Herzberg showed that several of the egoistic needs are of key importance as "satisfiers," and that achievement is one of the key motivators. Likert discovered system 4—a system of management dependent largely on satisfying egoistic needs. He said theory Y is essential to such a system. And finally McClelland appeared very close to finding out how to develop in people the need for achievement that may lead to greater success.[7]

Literally hundreds of man-years of effort have gone into the research of these behavioral scientists. Now we are witnessing a breakthrough in human motivation that may well change the world in which we live.

7. For further, highly interesting reading about these developments, *Motivation and Productivity,* by Saul Gellerman, is recommended (New York: The World Publishing Company, 1966). This book is well written and easy to read.

8 Training

One of the most challenging responsibilities any supervisor faces is the task of providing the proper training for his people. He can scarcely expect top performance if their knowledge or skill is not up to the demands of the work they must do. The better trained his people are, the more productive they can be, both individually and collectively.

Now it is obvious that any employee working at a job gains experience, that is to say, he learns. Putting this another way, an employee is taught or trained by the experiences in which he participates. These experiences may be accidental, in which case the man's training proceeds no faster than the experiences happen to occur. Or these experiences can be planned and arranged in such a way as to provide for steady, directed development of knowledge and skill. In both situations the man learns, but in the planned situation he has the opportunity to learn much more rapidly and correctly.

Training is the process of teaching, informing, or educating people (1) so that they may become as well qualified as possible to do their work, and (2) so that they may become qualified to perform in positions of greater difficulty and responsibility. Training has to be a two-way process. Someone must teach; someone must learn. Obviously the problem of training is the age-old problem of learning, or education.

Ordinarily we may think of education as the formal part of the learning process, which takes place in school. By training we usually mean that part of the learning process devoted to developing proficiency in a particular job or in a particular organization. When we train someone, we usually have in mind a very specific objective, attainable in a relatively short time, in contrast to "education," which is ordinarily much broader in scope and longer in development.

There are several schools of thought with respect to methods of training:

1. There is the "sink-or-swim" school, the members of which believe that the best way to train a man is to throw him into the work situation and let him sink or swim. In the University of Hard Knocks, they will tell you, the successful man will have learned, and learned well, what it takes to perform the job.

Learning by trial and error alone is usually considered a crude and wasteful way to learn. And yet the lessons learned by experience, as we say, seem to be firmly implanted in one's mind. We may be scornful of the method, even appalled at the waste it involves; yet we cannot deny the depth of the impressions resulting from it. Its principal drawbacks are its slowness and its waste of effort. As a device for introducing people to their jobs, it can be improved principally by stepping up its rate and reducing its waste. We cannot afford a lifetime to get a man into full operation on a job. But before we discard the method because of its extreme slowness, or because of its waste, we should certainly capitalize on its virtue —that of making deep and lasting impressions. If we can retain its virtues and correct its faults, the trial-and-error method of training can be of value.

2. Then there is the "send-him-out-with-Joe" school, the members of which believe that the best way to train a man is to put him under the wing of an experienced employee who will show him the ropes and teach him all he needs to know. This is the age-old apprenticeship system.

Properly used, this method can be a successful one, but unfortunately it is often not used skillfully. If Joe, the experienced worker, is a good teacher or trainer, and if he is really interested in training new men, and if he has enough time to devote to training (instead of production, which is his normal job), the apprenticeship approach can be valuable. Frequently enough, however, Joe is not a good teacher, and worse, he may resent being stuck with a new man. Joe, in fact, may be far more interested in doing his own job than in training new recruits. This last situation may be so because Joe is in a competitive situation, working against other experienced men in similar jobs to turn out the most and the best work.

At any rate, this method has more to recommend it than the sink-or-swim method. Generally, it is somewhat less costly than that method, and it is likely to train people more rapidly.

3. The third school is the Systematic school, the members of which believe (a) that training should be planned, scheduled, and systematically carried out; (b) that it should be based on the needs of the individual in relation to the demands of the job; and (c) that the best-known methods of teaching should be selectively used as they may apply.

There may be some of the apprenticeship method used, and in certain situations, a little of the sink-or-swim approach. But they will be used, along with many other methods, only where they are judged or have been found to be the best possible ways to get certain points across.

It is this systematic approach to training that can get the job done for the lowest cost. However, because of the variation in needs, plans, and people, such an approach can easily become overly elaborate. The impulse to add frills may prove almost overwhelming. And when this happens, supervisors may, in a revulsion of feeling, conclude that perhaps the old methods are best. This conclusion will be a natural one, however erroneous.

Kinds of Training

For our purposes, we may conveniently classify the many kinds of training into four general categories. Every supervisor needs to devote adequate attention to each of these four. These are:

1. Orientation training.
2. Job or production training.

3. Maintenance or refresher training.

4. Career or developmental training.

These four kinds of training merge freely into one another, and there is no particular virtue in trying to keep them meticulously segregated. Still, the training process ought to be undertaken in a certain order, and any supervisor ought to be aware of this sequence, as follows:

1. ORIENTATION TRAINING

This type of training is aimed at acquainting the new employee with his organization, his place in it, and the part he is expected to play in its work.

When a new man starts to work in an organization for the first time, he is eager to know what sort of an outfit he is getting into, what he is supposed to do, whom he will work with, and the like. His desire for knowledge and receptivity to training are possibly greater at this particular time than they may ever be again. He knows he is ignorant, so to speak, and his career depends on the acquiring of knowledge and skill. The new man feels great need for being shown what to do and how to do it. He is likely to be more attentive, more open-minded, and more eager than the experienced employees, who have already learned their work. What the new man learns in his earliest days in an organization is likely to remain indelibly fixed on his mind. Men on the verge of retirement often refer to their first days in the organization, which seem to stand out clearly in their minds, even after the passage of many years.

Orientation training is needed, without exception, by every new person who enters an organization. It is intended to *orient* the new employee, and the subject matter needs to include such things as are shown under supervisory Principle One on page 10. Orientation training is one obvious method for a supervisor to use in carrying out his responsibilities in supervision.

Notice we said that *every new person* entering an organization should be oriented. We stress this point since people in many agencies and companies seem to feel that a new clerk or messenger or typist should be trained only in his particular duties. These people do not understand the difference between a job and the start of a career. Nor do they realize that people work for more than the money they are paid. For a man to become a real and enthusiastic worker for his organization, he simply must know something about it, and feel a sense of pride in being part of it.

It is worth noting here too that orientation training in many government agencies and in many companies is performed by a training officer or his staff in special training classes. But this cannot relieve the supervisor of any responsibility whatever for the training of his own people. His new man may learn a great deal in the training class. But no such class can provide those personal details that orient the new man in *his* particular job, in *his* particular group of people, with *his* supervisor, and in the unique work situation to which he is assigned. Any supervisor needs to instruct his new men in such matters, preferably ahead of any orientation training class. Furthermore, it is of considerable importance that the supervisor check carefully to be sure his new people understand clearly what they were supposed to have learned in the training class.

2. JOB TRAINING

This type of training is aimed at teaching the employee how to do the job for which he was hired. The intent is to get the employee into full production in his job as soon as possible. For this reason, such training has often been called "production training." Its objective is to instill full understanding and knowledge of the job, and to teach the trainee *how* to perform all those activities that make up the work he is expected to do.

Job, or production, training is often mishandled. Frequently this comes about because a supervisor does not have clearly in mind either the objective of such training, the need for speed, or the best methods to use. Job training is by no means a simple matter, nor is it something to be handled by any single method. We can illustrate the situation by the following ideas:

Training costs money. *A completely untrained employee is the most expensive employee on the payroll,* since he is paid for practically no production at all. When he is at last fully trained, he is, as we say, *earning* his pay. All during the time he was not producing as fully as a well-trained man should, the cost of what he *did* produce was higher than it would have been with a trained man.

The first day a new man reports for work, he cannot earn his pay. He has to learn all about his job and how to do it before he can fully earn the salary attached to his position. Thus, from the time a man first enters on duty until just before he is finally producing fully in his job, he is actually not earning his full day's pay. Only after he is fully producing is he worth the salary paid him.

We can show this situation in a simple diagram, thus:

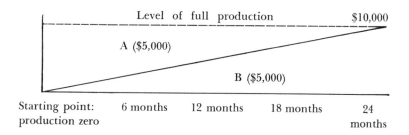

An untrained employee starts at zero; he produces noth-ing. Gradually he may learn by experience how to do the work involved in his job. Twenty-four months after he started to work, he has reached "full production"—that is, he is performing productively in all the duties he is expected to undertake. At the halfway point of twelve months, he is producing about half of what he will produce in another twelve months.

The triangular segment marked B represents the production of the employee. The segment marked A represents the area of no production. In other words, if, as the diagram shows, it takes the man two years to become fully productive, then the *total* production of the man during the two-year period is about half of what it would have been if the man had been fully trained to start with.

The new employee earns about half of the salary paid him during the two-year period. The other half he does not earn. If his salary were $5,000 per year, then the cost to the organization employing him to get him into full production is $10,000 in two years. In this same period, the learning employee earns half his salary, or $5,000. The other $5,000 goes for experience, or for his learning.

Suppose it were possible through systematic, intensive training to reduce the learning period in our hypothetical situation from twenty-four months to twelve. Our diagram would then look like this:

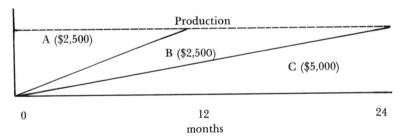

It is obvious on inspection of the diagram that area A has now been reduced in size (actually it has been cut in half), and that areas B and C together represent the productivity of the new man in a two-year period. In this situation he is now earning three-fourths of his $10,000, or $7,500; and there is a loss of only $2,500 (in area A).

Putting this another way: we can obviously well afford to spend up to $2,500 on the man's training, *if we can get him into full production in one year instead of two.* The less we have to spend, of course, the greater the profit we can hope to make. For example, $500 spent on training could get us a net profit of $2,000 in production. If the training cost is $1,000, the net profit is $1,500 in increased production. Thus we may conclude that the lower the cost of intensive training, the greater the profit to be realized in terms of the productivity of the employee. It should be clear, too, that *we must spend money on training to realize this profit,* and that if no money is spent, we lose the production anyway.

We would do even better if we could get the man into full production in six months. In this case we could afford to spend up to $2,500 plus $1,250 (half of A above), or $3,750, on his training. Each time we cut in half the time it takes to train him fully, we are able to spend one-half plus one-fourth, plus one-eighth, etc., of his annual salary. Note, however, that as the training times becomes shorter, the amounts we realize from speeding up the process become smaller.

The more intensive the training, the more difficult it is for the man to absorb it. There are practical limits to the learning ability of people. Many jobs require as much as two years for the employee to learn them. Most of these can be learned through intensive, systematized training in half that time, or possibly in one-fourth that time. Other jobs may take much less time to learn. Actually, the learning time for every job varies with the kind of job it is; each job requires study to determine the amount of time.

To illustrate what all this might mean, suppose we take an organization of ten thousand people with a yearly turnover in personnel of 10 percent. In such an organization there would be a thousand new people each year to train. Let us suppose that the average learning time for a new man is one year, but that with intensive training we would have him in full production in six months. If the average salary were $5,000, then we could afford to spend up to $1,250 per man for job training. This would amount to $1,250,000 for a thousand people per year. This amount is far in excess of what it need actually cost for the training. In such an organization as this—which is a reasonably common example—a possible profit of considerable size could be realized from such a training venture.

At any rate, it is clear that even though we consciously spend no money on systematic training, the learning period will cost money anyway. The amount is proportionate to the length of time it will take most people, on the average, to learn their jobs. The higher the salary a person gets, the greater the cost, or loss. It is possible to overspend on job training. A little analysis of training costs and results can often help reorient the program.

Supervisors must undertake job training with considerable care. Careless or indifferent handling of this training can result in far higher costs than necessary. Worse, it can result in employees lacking adequate training for their jobs. No organization can afford to use exclusively the philosophy of the sink-or-swim school, or the send-him-out-with-Joe school of thought. Nor is there too much truth in the belief that a man must be "seasoned," or left a long time in a job to "gain experience." The fact is that properly planned, skillfully handled instruction can turn out a well-trained employee *at a rate at least equal to the rate at which he can learn.* If, by seasoning, we mean primarily the development of wisdom in action, or improved judgment, then the constant application of trained intelligence to a variety of new problems can bring this about. This, too, can be planned and arranged.

3. MAINTENANCE OR REFRESHER TRAINING

Training of this kind is aimed at keeping people up to date, as well as enabling them to brush up on knowledge they have already received. Involved here are new ideas, new information, new methods, new techniques, and new developments, as well as reviews of older materials and ideas. Such training is needed both to help keep employees at the peak of their possible production and to prevent them from getting into a rut.

Refresher training takes place after job training has been pretty well completed. The objective here is literally to maintain knowledge levels. Too much refresher training can be wasteful, of course, but the need for its judicious, periodic application is clear. In one sense, the introduction of new ideas is not strictly refresher training in the proper sense of the phrase. That is why "maintenance training" is perhaps a better term.

Involved here too is the need for stimulating the employee to undertake his own self-improvement. If he has learned to continue his own education, he will be a far easier subject for maintenance training (and for the career training outlined next). Unfortunately, not all high school or college graduates have learned how to go on learning. Frequently enough, a supervisor must undertake to create in his man the desire for learning and for improving himself by his own efforts.

4. CAREER OR DEVELOPMENTAL TRAINING

This kind of training is devoted to developing and improving the knowledge, skills, and abilities of the employee, so that he may ultimately perform work of greater responsibility than his present position entails. Such training is not necessarily related to his immediate job. Rather, it is designed to broaden his knowledge and experience, and it may involve periodic testing to determine whether he has arrived at a point where he can accept and discharge responsibilities and perform in a position of greater difficulty than the one he holds.

Such training as this is difficult to come by in an organization that does not have a fully developed career system. It is relatively easy under a good career development policy. Even so, it requires thoughtful study by any supervisor of his people, their abilities, their ambitions, their interests, and their potentialities.

Here we come up against the idea that a man may, as we say, reach a "ceiling." We mean by this that we think he can go no farther, that he has developed about as far as he is able. No more career for him, at least vertically; he has reached his limit. And yet experience indicates that such an idea is so frequently untrue as to be a fallacy, more often than not. Too many people who (their supervisors thought) had "reached their ceiling" have gone on to much greater work and reached unsuspected heights in different and more challenging situations. Possibly the supervisor could not make the job challenging enough.

In career training, as in maintenance training, but to a much greater extent, there is need for stimulation of employee self-improvement. Career training becomes increasingly important as a man learns his job and does his work with increasing confidence and ease. An employee can be provided with opportunities, but in the end it is he himself who must make the most of them. Obviously, he who is prepared will make more out of an opportunity than he who is not.

Some Principles of Training

There are some half-dozen principles any supervisor needs to know and understand if he is to deal adequately with his training responsibilities. These principles, or important ideas, are listed below, as follows:

PRINCIPLE ONE

People must be interested in learning before they will accept training.

If the man does not really devote himself to his work because he enjoys it, training him is the more difficult. Moreover, the experienced man may feel that no one can teach him anything about his job, and that no one knows about the work as well as he does. This individual is often quite hard to train.

There are many reasons why a man may become interested in learning. Some men develop a love of knowledge for its own sake. Some are continually eager to learn because they are ambitious, because they believe in the organization for which they work, because they take pride in accomplishment, because they desire recognition for outstanding work performance, because they want to earn more money, or for many other reasons.

There is always the additional spur of the realization that the boss wants certain things done. If it is not clear that the boss expects the man to do a certain thing as a result of training, then possibly only the man's good-natured willingness is the motivation.

PRINCIPLE TWO

Training must be suited to the individual needs of those being trained.

Before teaching or training a man to perform any kind of work, the man's supervisor needs to evaluate what the man can already do and what he already knows. Once it is clear what his particular deficiencies are—and this is a highly individual matter—then a training program can be devised to help him correct these deficiencies. What we do is to fit the training program to the man instead of fitting the man to the training program. The training must be related to the job a man must do and to the performance standards for that job.

PRINCIPLE THREE

Training must be done either by a supervisor or under his direction.

A supervisor may personally teach his men, or he may arrange for someone else to do so. However the job is done, he cannot escape his personal responsibility, inherent in his supervisory job, for being sure that his people *are* well trained for their work.

This is part of the basic philosophy underlying all supervision. If people are to look to their supervisor for guidance and direction, he had better be there when he is needed. He must see that they learn their jobs, and that they are given every possible opportunity to grow in stature, so that they may undertake increasingly difficult work. If training is conducted by another person or by other means, without reference to the supervisor, the trainee tends to grow away from his supervisor. He becomes obligated, as it were, *not* to the supervisor, but to the outside source of his enlightenment. Always, a man must understand that however his training and development may be carried out, his supervisor is the man who planned it, arranged it, or gave it. An experienced and able supervisor, intent upon commanding the respect and loyalty of his people, will always be found closely associated and identified with their development.

A training officer cannot be made responsible for the training that should be conducted by the supervisor. The training officer properly has the job of helping and advising the supervisor on needs, methods, arrangements, and evaluation of results.

PRINCIPLE FOUR

The rate of training should equal the rate at which an individual can learn.

This principle would seem particularly applicable to new employees. After all, nothing is to be gained by proceeding at a snail's pace when it is possible to go forward more rapidly. In fact, the slower the rate of training in relation to the learning ability of an individual, the more wasteful it is. Capable teachers will tell you that some students learn faster than others, and that those who can learn rapidly deserve special attention. So it is also with new employees. The sooner they can achieve full productivity, the sooner they earn their full salary, and the sooner the organization stops losing money while they learn.

But this principle is equally applicable to career training. Every job in a company or government agency becomes vacant, sooner or later, and often unexpectedly. The more men there are who are ready to assume greater responsibility, the more likelihood there is that the vacancy will be filled with a qualified man. In large organizations particularly, the number of positions of responsibility available may often become somewhat greater than the supply of well-trained people. Thus career training conducted at a rate consistent with learning ability is not only advisable but necessary.

PRINCIPLE FIVE

People can learn by being told or shown how to do work, but best of all from doing work under guidance.

There are those who can "talk" a good fight. And it is frequently said that "book learning cannot substitute for experience." Experience, we say, is the best teacher. But experience can be misleading, too, if it is the wrong kind, so that careful guidance of experience would seem to be wise.

What the principle leads to is the idea that while oral instruction or demonstration can reduce a period of trial-and-error fumbling, in the end the person being trained must actually perform the job. It is during performance that he really learns what he must do in order to continue performing successfully.

PRINCIPLE SIX

Training should be planned, scheduled, executed, and evaluated systematically.

It may be that we have several principles here, all combined into one, but since the process of training ought to be continuous, we may consider these four phases together.

1. *Planning.* As has already been implied, a training plan should contain a list of the ideas and skills that are essential to the job for which a man is to be trained. In addition, it should indicate the approximate time required, on the average, for the total training. In making such a list and timetable, it is important to avoid either oversimplification or over-elaboration of the training items. It is possible to subdivide the list into a series of ideas or skills so detailed in character as to obscure the essentials in which training is needed.

Obviously, a general plan can be made for any job without reference to an individual employee. It is when the listings are compared with the man's skills and abilities that the plan becomes significant for any given individual.

2. *Scheduling.* Tentative completion dates should be indicated for each item in the training plan. These dates should be set after due consideration of the total time ordinarily required and of any seasonal or other factors likely to affect the schedule. The schedule can later be adjusted to fit the rate at which the man learns.

3. *Execution.* As the training plan is carried out, the trainer or trainers can use the plan, including the schedule, as a check list. Appropriate notes can be included on each item, indicating satisfactory completion, need for additional work, and the like.

4. *Evaluation.* Failure to evaluate the results of training is possibly one of the commonest of all faults of training programs. It is not enough to *give* the training, however well-planned, scheduled, and conducted. *In the end we must ascertain whether the training was successful.* Workshops, conferences, or training meetings aimed at improving employee understanding or performance simply cannot be evaluated by asking the men how they liked the session. The question is really not whether they found the conference interesting, boring, stimulating, or tiresome. Rather, the question is, What did each participating employee learn? The

employees may agree that it was a "splendid session," a "fine meeting," or "one of the best they ever attended." But *unless they learned* what was being taught, the session was a flat failure.

There are several direct ways of finding out what the trainees learned, that is, of evaluating the training. These ways are well known to teachers, as follows:

1. Oral or written tests are given to ascertain whether the trainee has learned what he has been told or has been assigned to read. These tests need not be elaborate, but they should establish beyond doubt whether the man has the required knowledge of the subject.

2. Actual performance is observed by the trainer to determine whether the man has developed the ability and the skill to do the required work. Obviously, the performance cannot be guided, nor should the man be coached when the testing is going on. Guiding and coaching are used while the man is being taught. When he is being tested, he is on his own.

3. The work done by a trainee is reviewed after a time (short periods at first, longer ones later) to check the quantity and quality of results. This type of evaluation ordinarily comes after items 1 and 2 above, and continues thereafter as long as the man stays in the position. Test results of all kinds can well be noted in the training plan.

Exactly how plans and schedules are made and executed and how training is evaluated is a matter of choice with the supervisor. The important point is that the training job be done in a systematic way, with an objective clearly in view, and that its results be carefully checked upon its conclusion.

The Device of the Training Plan

At this point it is worthwhile to describe a simple working device that has proved generally useful to supervisors. This is a *written* training plan.

A supervisor who has never made one of these will find, if he tries it, that his job becomes much better organized. After all, it is difficult to keep in mind all the many things a new man must learn. It is much easier to jot them down in a list. And if the plan is developed *with the trainee participating,* the training itself tends to gain significance.

Such a plan can be developed in many ways. One useful approach is as shown below. Use a plain sheet of paper, and head columns something like this:

1	2	3	4	5	6	7
Job or activity		Who will do the training	When it will be done	How	Where	Remarks
1.						
2.						
3.						
4.						
5.						

Inspection of this beginning page of such a plan shows how it may be used. Column 1 carries a complete listing of all the things a man must know and be able to do in the job he is entering. This listing can be prepared for any job well in advance—provided the duties of the job are clear and well understood.

Column 2 is simply checked if the man already knows or can do the specific item. If it is blank for any activity, then we use the following columns.

Column 3 carries the name of the person who will do the training. The supervisor can put his own initials here, whenever he intends to do the training himself.

Column 4 can indicate conveniently the dates when the training will take place. Or a single date can show the deadline by which time the item should be completed, e.g., "by June 15." And, better show the year!

Column 5 should show how the training will be done. The entries might read: "conference," "reading assignment," "on the job," and the like.

Column 6 shows where the training will take place. For example, a training conference might be held in Denver. An on-the-job bit of training might be done in the "office."

Column 7 is used to indicate that training on any item is completed satisfactorily—or that additional training is needed. If the latter is true, it can be added at the end of the list, for renewed effort.

This plan is developed with the trainee himself, and is given to him to keep. *No copies* need be made.[1] As the training progresses, the supervisor asks his trainee to bring in his training plan, and appropriate entries are made on it. Additional items will probably need to be put in the plan—which thus becomes open-ended. Experience in various organizations suggests that such a plan has a useful life of perhaps as much as two years. After that, keeping it up may become somewhat of a chore. Experience also indicates that formalizing this plan—on a printed form, with copies to various places—tends to diminish its value. Nor does it need to be typed.

Training Methods

There are many ways to go about teaching people, and they vary with the student and the teacher. No one can say generally that one method is better than another. The question is how effective the method is with the man or men being trained. Listed below are some of the better-known methods as suggestions for the consideration of supervisors.

1. ASSIGNED READING

This is most useful in connection with a job requiring knowl-

1. If you don't like excessive paperwork, don't make it!

edge that must be utilized for performance. Assigned reading would ordinarily be somewhat less useful with simpler work, for example filing, or message-carrying. Even here, however, assigned reading can be useful in giving the employee an explanation of the agency in which he works and the importance of his task in relation to the whole. As always, the trainer needs to ascertain by testing whether the man understands what he has read.

Reading is also essential for maintenance and career training, and it is one of the important devices used to broaden the horizon of men as they develop. No professional person can keep up to date in his field, nor can he increase his knowledge and perspective, without extensive reading. This has become increasingly true as the world's knowledge has grown, and as books, journals, and magazines have been published in constantly growing quantity.

A man's reading must necessarily change with his jobs. If, for example, he begins his career as an engineer, it is appropriate that he read material on engineering. But should he become a supervisor, then he should turn to the best that has been written in the fields of supervision, management, and administration. All too frequently, the technician-turned-administrator fails to realize the extent of the literature available in his new field of effort. This literature requires as much searching, selection, and study as does that in any technical field.

2. INDIVIDUAL COUNSELING AND GUIDANCE

This method of teaching includes techniques usable by a master and his apprentice or by the tutor and the student. But as used in job training, for example, it may possibly include something more.

In the first place, a supervisor (the trainer, in this case) must observe his man in the performance of his work. In doing this, he makes mental or written notes of the things the trainee does that need improvement.

Second, the trainer discusses the observed performance fully, commending the good things, and suggesting ways of improving items that are in need of it.

Third, and later on, he again observes the trainee's performance to ascertain whether the suggestions have been taken up and used.

This simple three-step procedure is capable of considerable variation. For example, rather than *suggest* an improvement, the supervisor may *demonstrate* by performing the work himself. Also, in situations where a supervisor is guiding a number of people, he is well advised to take written notes on the suggestions he makes, keeping a copy himself and giving one to his trainee. This is simply for the purpose of reminding himself (and the trainee) later on as to what the suggestions actually were. Where many trainees are involved, it is quite easy to confuse both performance and suggestions unless they are committed to writing.

3. GROUP TRAINING

This method of approach presumes that all the people in the group need or want to be trained in the same thing. For example, a half-dozen new recruits all need to know about the organization they have just joined. In this case, the group method is obviously appropriate and is less time-consuming for the teacher than covering the same ground with each man individually.

The reason why there are classes in any school is that a great many more teachers would be required to deal with each student on an individual basis. Instead, one teacher is able to talk to a class, develop discussions between the students and himself, undertake demonstrations that can be observed by all students at once, and test what has been learned by questioning or observing later performance. Even in the classroom, however, the teacher must devote as much time as he can to each student individually. When the ratio between teachers and students is large, the individual attention per student may be small—sometimes so small as to be unsatisfactory, at least for certain students.

In recent years a great deal of material has been published on conference methods, some of which has value for the supervisor who is undertaking maintenance training with his group. With due allowance for some of the unimportant frills that have crept in, the supervisor can profit by a study of the general principles of holding conferences. Possibly one of the most important of the techniques suggested is that of gaining participation in discussion by *all* members of the group. This technique is simple and, indeed, requires only thoughtful observation on the part of the chairman, but it is often neglected.

The leader of a group being trained needs to make use of various visual aids. Blackboards are obvious. Large-sized pads of paper are especially useful if a record must be kept. Pictures, photographs, slides, motion pictures, flannelboards, tackboards, recordings, and other devices may also be used where they are needed. But the devices should be kept commensurate with the subject matter. It is worth recalling that the greatest teachers the world has ever known had none of these.

9   *Communications*

Every day a supervisor has to make himself understood by his people, and every day he has to try to understand what they are attempting to convey to him. This two-way process is usually labeled *communication,* and a great deal depends on it. If a supervisor and his people cannot or do not communicate very well, the work they must perform will suffer accordingly. This need for communication is not confined to the field of supervision; it poses the same problem in any field of endeavor. Wherever people are trying to do something together—build a bridge, run a government, or establish world peace—what they get done depends on how well they understand each other.

People have been *mis*understanding each other for a long time. Misunderstanding can easily lead to dislike, enmity, or hatred, and it has frequently led to war between nations. It is far wiser for a supervisor to think carefully about *his own skill* in conveying and receiving ideas than it is to assume, without thinking, that he already knows all he needs to know about the subject.

There are two important ways by which people communicate, that is, convey ideas to one another. They do it by talking and listening. Or they do it by writing and reading. In both of these processes, one person sends a message and another person receives it. In both the processes, the sending and receiving require considerable skill.

The principal trouble in this matter of communicating is that so many people think it is really no problem at all. Talking and listening and reading and writing are usually thought of as things everyone knows how to do. And there is a certain amount of truth in this belief. However, each of these skills has to be studied and learned, and one does not necessarily learn them by going to school. Many supervisors have failed because they assumed that any or all of the following simple statements were true:

1. Anyone who talks plainly to another person will always be understood.

2. Anyone can listen to another person talking and easily understand his meaning.

3. Anyone can write what he means on paper, and his meaning will be understood by anyone else who reads it.

4. Anyone can read what someone else has written and understand what the writer meant.

All these statements are dangerous generalizations. They are not "trick" statements, nor are they intended to contain any "hidden" meaning. All of them assume perfectly ordinary situations involving the language we use every day. The statements imply that talking and listening and reading and writing are usually quite simple skills you learn more or less as you grow up—at home, in school, among your friends.

It is dangerous, however, to take these four skills for granted. Many books have been written about language, its uses, its weaknesses, and its deceptions. The interested supervisor may find it worthwhile to review some of these books, which treat the subject more fully than we can do here.[1] For our purposes, we will discuss four aspects of communicating in a way that may be most practical for the supervisor. The four aspects are these:

1. A supervisor must be able to speak clearly.

2. He must be able to listen.

3. He must be able to write clearly.

4. He must be able to read with understanding.

1. S. I. Hayakawa, *Language in Thought and Action* (New York: Harcourt, Brace, Jovanovich, 1949); Stuart Chase, *Tyranny of Words* (New York: Harcourt, Brace, Jovanovich, 1938); Stuart Chase, with Marian Tyler Chase, *Roads to Agreement* (New York: Harper & Row, 1951); and Alfred Korzybski, *Science and Sanity* (4th ed., Lakeville, Conn.: International Non-Aristotelian Library, 1958).

Talking-Listening

Of the two skills involved in the talking-listening process, most people seem to have the greatest trouble with listening. They assume that listening is the same thing as hearing, and that anyone who can hear can therefore listen. (And it is true that if your hearing is impaired, you will have more difficulty listening than a normal person will.) But listening, as we are using the word here, requires not only that you hear, but also that you understand what you hear. To do this you must *think about* what you hear another person say when he is talking to you. Actually, your speaker may not be skillful at all in getting his ideas across.

The key to successful listening is to be an active, *demanding listener*. The idea is that you try as hard as you can to be sure you understand correctly what a speaker is trying to tell you. This means that you cannot be thinking of what *you* are going to say as soon as your speaker pauses for breath. Instead, you think about *his* meaning. This takes some effort if you have not tried it before—and many people have not. We are often so anxious to get our own ideas across that we try to do all the talking, and hence we miss what others want to tell us. We need to devote our *whole* attention to the business of listening.

Now it happens that scientists have developed some valuable and important ideas about listening. This has been done notably by psychologists and by specialists in general semantics, which has to do with the relation between language and human behavior. The semanticists suggest that there are three key questions a good listener should keep in mind as he listens to a speaker. We list them first, then discuss each one. Here they are:

1. What does the speaker mean, i.e., what is he trying to say?

2. How does he know, i.e., what evidence has he for what he is trying to say?

3. What is he leaving out?

1. WHAT DOES THE SPEAKER MEAN?

Several ideas are important to bear in mind here. In the first place we need to realize that the meaning of the speaker is *not* in the words he uses. You simply cannot assume that he uses words exactly the same way you do. He uses them *his* way, and he is different from you. The meaning is in the speaker, not in the words. Therefore you start your listening with the idea that you do not know what the speaker's words mean to him—and you must spare no pains to find out. Probe. Ask questions: "Do I understand you to mean . . . ?" "Is this what you are saying . . . ?" "If I understand you correctly, you mean . . ." Tell him in your own words what you think he meant in order to find out whether you understood him correctly.

It is important to check your understanding when the speaker is using what we think of as ordinary, simple words that are nontechnical. It is usually safe to assume you understand correctly when a speaker uses a technical word—providing you know its meaning. For example, if he talks about sodium chloride, you may be sure he is talking about table salt, since sodium chloride is the chemical term for table salt—and *it has no other meaning*. But for the commonly used words there are many meanings. For example, if I tell you that I saw an interesting tie the other day, you do not know whether I am talking about a necktie, a football game, a tie on a railroad track, or something else. We are told on good authority that the five hundred most-used words in the English language have a total of some fourteen thousand meanings as listed in the Oxford English Dictionary.

2. HOW DOES THE SPEAKER KNOW?

This question does not imply that you should take a challenging position with the speaker. Instead, you try to find out the basis for what he is telling you. You look for the facts, the evidence, behind what the speaker is saying. You ask more questions. How did you learn this? Why do you say this? How do you know? Can you show me?

You ask such questions diplomatically, after your speaker has finished what he has to say. What you want, remember, is to understand what the speaker means. To help you do this, you are trying to discover how correct and how factual his statements are.

3. WHAT IS THE SPEAKER LEAVING OUT?

It may occur to you at this point to wonder how you can possibly listen for something that is not spoken. And here we have an important difference between hearing and listening. You cannot, of course, hear what is not said. But as you listen, you may realize that your speaker is leaving a number of things unsaid. He may leave out important facts and details. He may favor one conclusion when you can see that there are several others. And he may not see or say anything about the implications of the conclusion he does favor. All this takes work on your part. But remember, we pointed out in the beginning that successful listening cannot be passive; it must be demanding and, hence, active.

Some General Rules About Listening

In addition to the three questions a skilled listener needs to keep in mind and use, there are a few general rules that can also help him listen. Most of these come to us from the psychologists. The rules are not difficult to observe, although they are widely neglected.

First of all, it is important to *relax* when you are listening. If you strain too hard, you are likely to find it correspondingly harder to understand. Extensive, controlled experiments by the United States Navy during the last war with airplane personnel confirmed this idea, which had long been held by the psychologists.

These same Navy experiments showed, too, that a second

general rule was important, a rule that the professional psychologists have been using for many years, especially since the time of Dr. Sigmund Freud. This rule is: *hear the speaker out.* Let him talk until he is finished. Do not cut him off. Do not contradict him. Do not start looking out the window. Listen actively and carefully to what he says, all the way through. Then, start asking your questions. This simple approach often has the effect of helping a speaker to say more plainly what he means. To find his listener actually waiting until he is finished is likely to be flattering to him. He finds that you seem *interested* in what he has to say, and he will work all the harder to be sure you understand his meaning.

This leads us to a third general rule, which embodies a familiar method of the psychologists. This is to listen patiently, without criticizing, passing judgment, or giving advice. The idea is to let the man speak as freely and fully as possible, without fear of censure or blame. This procedure is known to psychologists and psychiatrists as *nondirective counseling.* The listener has to be patient. He usually confines his remarks to restating what the speaker has said, in slightly different words. This causes the speaker to feel not only that he is being listened to, but he is truly being understood. When the speaker gets through, you most specifically do not tell him you think he is wrong, or stupid, or foolish, or prejudiced—even if you think so. Instead, you go ahead using your three questions.

The fourth general rule is an interesting one. It is that in order to listen well, *one must disregard symbols of authority* as such. We cannot listen effectively if we are overawed or impressed by a speaker's title, or name, or rank, or academic degree, or uniform, or wealth, or position. These things are not necessarily evidence that what he is saying is reliable or valid. You evaluate the statements as usual, patiently hearing him out, then using your three questions. In the words of Wendell Johnson, whose ideas we have been using liberally here

The quality of his (the speaker's) voice, the color of his skin, the slant of his eyes, his height, weight, and apparent age guarantee nothing with respect to the wisdom or foolishness of what he says. Truth can be lisped, stuttered, or twanged through the nose just as well as it can be molded by a meticulous Harvard or Oxford tongue. It can be mispronounced. It may be ungrammatical. Whether it comes in a satin case or a paper bag is a matter of no importance. To a general semanticist, the Men of Distinction are first of all, and often solely, just colored pictures. The art of listening involves realistic appraisal of the conventional symbols of authority, as such.[2]

The Other Half of the Talking-Listening Process

Let us now put ourselves in the position of the speaker. Let us assume that when we speak, our listeners are going to be active, demanding listeners, bent on trying to understand us. Now, what can we do to bring about the best possible communication? (We are discussing the way a speaker talks to one or two people, remember, not to a large audience.)

Clearly, we need to *think about* our listeners, and be just as active in trying to get our meaning across as they will be in trying to understand us. Our listeners will hear us out— so, we are as brief as the subject matter permits. We speak with care, choosing our words well, clarifying each point as well as we are able. Since our listeners will want the evidence for our statements, we take pains to provide it. We try for truth as objectively as we can. Our listeners will be watching for what we leave out, so we try for completeness in our statements from beginning to end. In every way possible to us, we try to think of our audience, that is, our listeners, and how likely it is that they are getting the meaning of what we are trying to say.

All this is no more than using the ideas about listening in reverse. But there are some other things we know that can help us when we are doing the talking. The same Navy ex-

2. Wendell Johnson, "Do You Know How to Listen?", *Etc.*, Autumn 1949, pp. 3–9.

periments mentioned earlier also brought out some useful points about talking. They showed, for example, that speakers who talked too fast did not get across as well as those who spoke more slowly. This was especially true when the speakers were using simpler, more commonly used words. It helped also if speakers made a real effort to talk in short sentences, and to use patterns of inflection or tones of voice that would help to bring out meaning. From these experiments we can say that (1) speakers should avoid talking too fast, (2) they should use plain and simple words as much as possible, (3) they should speak in shorter, rather than longer, sentences, and (4) they should use the inflection of their voices to lend emphasis and clarity. Speakers cannot do these things unless they *think before they speak.*

Further helps to speakers trying for good communication come from Irving Lee. In his book *How to Talk with People*[3] he suggests a number of things speakers would do well to *avoid.* Some of these are:

1. Try to avoid bluntly contradicting those with whom you are talking. You should be trying for understanding, not just to make your listeners angry.

2. It is unwise to use inflammatory words or to descend to name-calling. If you say or imply that a man is a fool, he is likely to get angry. If you call him any kind of nasty name or otherwise insult him, you will usually get the same effect. This does not help communication at all; it only defeats it.

3. Try to avoid generalities whenever it is possible to be specific. For example, you may have had a bad experience with two women supervisors, but you cannot therefore generalize that all women supervisors are no good. You can, however, state that with two particular women supervisors whom you have observed, your experience was not good.

4. Try not to sound *final* in your statements. Put them on a tentative basis, and say or imply that you are still looking for a better conclusion. For example, if you say, "This is the

3. New York: Harper & Row, 1952.

only way we can do this," you may arouse more argument than if you say, "So far, this way looks pretty good, but possibly another way may have occurred to you."

5. Try not to "talk down" to your listeners. If you give the impression that you think you know all there is to know about a subject, your listeners may form the opinion that you are conceited or overconfident. This does not help understanding.

6. You personally, as a speaker, will do well to avoid becoming angry at your listeners. Likewise, you should avoid feeling that if a man disagrees with you he is therefore either a fool or stupid. And keep in mind that when a man differs with you, he is not necessarily conducting a personal attack on your integrity.

7. Avoid using the "hard approach" rather than the "soft approach." Introduce your critical or contradictory statements with such simple phrases as "I wonder if we could look at it this way . . . You may be right, but would you be willing to consider . . . ? You may know more about this than I, and I hesitate to say, but . . . I realize you have a very good point, although perhaps we might look at it this way . . ." Studies of arguments in conferences made by Irving Lee indicate pretty clearly that the "gentle phrase" or soft approach tends to reduce markedly people's resistance to criticism. On the other hand, the blunt, hard approach tends to ruffle the listeners' feelings—and agreement becomes more difficult to reach.

One of our ablest diplomats, Benjamin Franklin, had some things to say about this "soft approach." He used it with great skill, and his *Autobiography* notes in one place:

The way to convince another is to state your case moderately and accurately. Then scratch your head, or shake it a little and say that is the way it seems to you, but that, of course, you may be mistaken about it. This causes your listener to receive what you have to say, and, as like as not, turn about and try to convince you of it, since you are in doubt. But if you go at him in a tone of positiveness and arrogance, you only make an opponent of him.

This soft approach must be sincere. Lee's simple studies showed that this approach made some difference about two-thirds of the time. And he suggests that if you do not get results in a given situation, why, discard it for other methods.

The Writing-Reading Process

We are not concerned here with writing or reading literary masterpieces. Our intent is to discuss some simple ways of writing and reading that may help us in communicating with each other. No more. Anyone of ordinary intelligence who is able to read and write can learn these simple methods.

Many experts have worked on the problem of making writing as readable as possible. All of them have approached the problem on somewhat the same basis. They have taken sizable groups of people and tested their comprehension of different types of written material. They ascertained the kind of writing that was easily understood by people with a fifth-grade education, sixth-grade, seventh-grade, and so on, up through college. People who have graduated from grammar school, that is, the eighth grade, in general can read much more difficult material than can those who stopped their education at lower grades. High school graduates can read—with ease—more difficult material than can be easily and comfortably read by eighth-grade graduates. College graduates can do still better. On the basis of many years of study of hundreds of people and their reading comprehension, various formulas have been developed. These formulas can be used to classify most kinds of written material.

We use here a formula developed by Robert Gunning, a communications expert, in his book *The Technique of Clear Writing*.[4] His formula is not necessarily the best, but it is by all odds the simplest to use. The Gunning formula enables you to arrive at what he calls the "Fog Index." The higher the index, the more "fog" there is in the written material. The lower the Fog Index, the less "fog" there is. Gunning's

4. New York: McGraw-Hill Book Co., 1952.

formula offers a quick way to estimate how easy or how hard any piece of writing is. This is the way you use it:

1. Count off 100 words in the written material you want to test. Do not use a larger sample than this, because the formula doesn't work if you do. Make a mark at the end of the hundredth word. If the material is long, you will have to take several samples, say at every tenth page or hundredth page.

2. Figure the average length of sentence in the 100-word sample. Stop with the sentence that ends nearest (either before or after) the 100-word mark. For example, if two sentences make up 104 words, then the average sentence length would be 52 words. If there are ten sentences in 96 words, the average length is 96 divided by 10 or 9.6 words.

3. Next we find the percentage of "hard words." To do this we count the number of "hard words"—which Gunning calls words of three syllables or more—in the 100-word sample. (The word "next" has one syllable; "number" has two; "syllable" has three.) In doing this, do not count capitalized words, such as Paris, London, President, etc. Do not count words that are combinations of short, easy words (like book-keeper or white-collar). And do not count words that have a third syllable when *ed* or *es* is added to them (like *expected* or *refuses*).

4. Last you do the figuring. Since we have a 100-word sample, the number of hard words can be used directly as the percentage figure. First, add the number of hard words to the average sentence length. Then multiply the sum by 0.4. This will give you the Fog Index. The factor of 0.4 relates the sum to school-grade reading level. You may take our word for it that the formula really works, even if you do not understand why. If you are interested in the theory behind the formula, read Gunning's book mentioned above.

Now let us apply this yardstick. We will take a piece out of a bulletin on supervision. We have underscored the hard words:

There is need also for much additional basic and applied research: research to determine the major duties of supervisor's jobs, the differences among them, and the situations which help determine the qualifications needed, and to develop new methods for evaluation; and applied research to test the validity of new and existing selection methods on the supervisors of many different types of supervisory positions. Much more than half of the total research work reported here is based on supervisors of blue-collar workers, an important group, but far from being the only group for whom supervisory selection is important. The organization of. . . .

Our line here stops us at the end of 100 words.

This passage contains 97 words through the sentence that ends nearest the 100-word mark. There are two sentences. So we divide 97 by 2 to get 48.5. All the words underscored add up to 22 hard words. (Note we did not count "report*ed*" or "blue-collar.")

Now we do our simple calculation:

$$
\begin{array}{rl}
\text{Add} \quad & 48.5 \quad \text{(average sentence length)} \\
& +\,22 \quad \text{(hard words)} \\
\hline
\text{Total} \quad & 70.5 \\
\text{Multiply by} \quad & \times \;\, 0.4 \\
\hline
\end{array}
$$

28.20—the Fog Index

As it happens, there simply is no twenty-eighth grade in school. Our sample indicates that the writing would be hard to read for everyone, regardless of his school education. The writer must expect to find that his readers will be few, and of these few, only a handful may spend the time and effort required to understand what he meant.

Before you smile at this example, better test some of your own writing—one of your letters, a memorandum, or something else you have written. Many people are shocked to discover that they habitually write with a Fog Index far above college reading level. Certainly a great many memorandums have a Fog Index of 20 to 30, which means that the people who must read them have considerable difficulty understanding them. Worse, when especially difficult memorandums are completely misunderstood—as they so frequently are—the activities involved may become very badly snarled. Test some of the instructional material you get from time to time. Test an article or two of the *Reader's Digest* or *Ladies' Home Journal,* which scale their articles to reach large numbers of educated adults.

In the following table you can see how the Fog Index relates to reading level. The figures in the third column give the percentage of people in the United States who have reached the grades shown. For example, 88 percent of us have had at least an eighth-grade education, and we can read with ease any material with a Fog Index of 8 or less. Note that even college graduates can read such material with ease, not just grammar school graduates.

Fog Index	Reading Level by Grade	Percent of People Reaching Grade	Medial School Years Completed
17	College graduate	3.5	
16	College senior	9.5	
15	College junior	11.6	
14	College sophomore	16.6	
13	College freshman	21.0	
12	High school senior	53.6	12.1
11	High school junior	61.6	
10	High school sophomore	67.9	
9	High school freshman	75.0	
8	Eighth grade	87.8	
7	Seventh grade		
6	Sixth grade		
5	Fifth grade	96.1	

Younger people generally have had more education than older people. And men generally have had a little more education than women, except that many more women than men have had four years of high school.

Now we might get back to our sample and try making it easier to read. In doing this we are somewhat handicapped because we are not sure exactly what the writer meant. *He* could have done a much better job than we can do. Here is a rewrite, with the hard words underscored as before:

We need more research. We need to know the major duties of supervisor's jobs and how they differ. We must know what qualifications a supervisor should have for any given situation. We must learn how to judge these. We need to study how valid our selection methods are with supervisors, in many kinds of jobs. Most of the research reported here has to do with supervisors of blue-collar workers. This is an important group, but it is far from being the only group for whom supervisory selection is important.

As rewritten, the sample now contains 89 words. There are seven sentences, so the average sentence length is 89 divided by 7, or 12.7. There are 11 hard words, that is, 11 out of 89 words are three-syllable words. We divide 11 by 89 to get the percentage, which is 12. We apply our formula thus:

Add	12.7	(average sentence length)
	+ 12	(percentage of hard words)
Total	24.7	
Multiply by	× 0.4	

9.88—the Fog Index

If the rewritten sample correctly expresses what the writer had in mind (which we do not know), then the written material is now easy and comfortable reading for anyone who has finished two years of high school. As such, it would probably be read by far more people, with greater understanding, than our original sample with a Fog Index of 28.2.

Notice, by the way, that we made no special effort to be brief. The rewritten piece happened to come out a little shorter than the original, but it might just as well have been longer. What we are saying is that ease of reading is more important than being brief, if brevity results in hard reading.

We may now draw some conclusions about communication by writing, based on the use of a Fog Index, as follows:

1. Just as a speaker must try to express himself as clearly as he can for his listener's sake, so must a writer do likewise for the sake of his readers. A writer has an even harder task because his readers cannot ask him questions about what he meant. They can only ponder what he wrote.

2. Supervisors who must write letters or memorandums— or who must sign material written by others for them—should have some means of judging how readable they will be. Gunning's Fog Index is one way this can be done. Another excellent method is explained by Rudolf Flesch, and this one also deserves careful study.[5]

3. Because short sentences and simple words make reading easier, writers need to *think about* that fact *as they write*. You will find, after a little practice, that you can indeed produce more easily readable material. But this does take conscious effort. It means also that when you write, you have two jobs to do. First, your subject matter must be correct. Second, the way it is written has to be consciously scaled to the reading level of your readers.

A Note About Brevity

Many supervisors or administrators habitually demand that reports, letters, and memos be brief and to the point. "Give it to me in one page. Condense it to a single paragraph," they say. We can sympathize with such requests, because we may know that the executive is busy and that there are many demands on his time. However, if you are one of these brief-and-to-the-point people, better consider whether you are getting what you really want. You just may be getting brevity

5. Rudolf Flesch, *The Art of Readable Writing* (New York: Harper & Row, 1949). This book is a lot of fun to read. Furthermore, it's tremendously helpful to anyone trying to improve the clarity of his writing.

at the expense of understanding.

For example, consider the following sentence. It is brief and to the point: "*Condensation diminishes comprehension.*"

The Fog Index of this item is 41.2. (There are three words in the sentence. The percentage of hard words is 100—they're *all* hard words. Thus, $100 + 3 \times 0.4 = 41.2$.)

That sentence is harder to understand than the following: "*If you condense things too much, people will have a hard time understanding what you mean.*"

The Fog Index of this item is 8.8. (There are 16 words in the sentence. The percentage of hard words is one in 16, or 6.2. Thus $16 + 6.2 \times 0.4 = 8.8$.)

Possibly the solution is to provide the hard-pressed executive with written material that is complete and understandable. But put a summary at the very beginning. If he is interested in the summary, then he can read further, if he has time.

Some Ideas on Reading

We now come to consider the other half of the writing-reading process, that is, the business of trying to understand written material. In doing this we cannot do more than accord thoughtful and careful attention to it. There is no chance, ordinarily, to ask the writer what he meant. Of course, it is always possible to write a letter to an author or to the office the memorandum came from. This takes extra time, and sometimes you may not realize that you have misread the material. What we are emphasizing here is that when you *read* something, give it your full and critical attention. Think of the three questions you would ask of a speaker, restated as: (1) What does the writer mean? (2) What is the evidence for what he has written? (3) What has the writer left out? These may help you to understand what is on the page.

But there is far more to reading than the critical study

aspect. So much material comes in printed or mimeographed form—books, bulletins, magazines, newspapers, memorandums, handbooks, manuals, letters, etc. Almost anyone trying to keep up with what is going on in the world, and in his own organization, is likely to get a little desperate about it. And there seems so little time to digest it all.

For the slow reader the situation seems hopeless. He just cannot seem to read fast enough to get through half the things he ought to. Or so he thinks. The fact is that people who can read rapidly were not born that way. They have *developed* their skill. Anyone who can read at all can learn to read more rapidly providing he is trained or trains himself to do it. What this takes is the application of a little common sense plus practice.

Sorting

The common-sense angle has to do with sorting out what you really *need* to read. Sorting is really an organized approach to reading. It is often more important to a busy man than his ability to read rapidly.

You most certainly do *not* need to read everything that happens to come your way, word for word. A great deal of written stuff is not worth your time. Some of it may be. So a few minutes spent sorting the wheat from the chaff can save you possibly hours of valuable time later on. As a suggestion, you can easily sort reading material into groups like these:

1. *The material you don't need to read at all.* This may include instructions that do not apply in any way to *your* work. It may include books or bulletins that are of no value to you. It certainly includes a great deal of material in any daily newspaper—all the classified ads, all the death notices, and so on. This is the kind of material that simply is not important to you. Best advice is to get rid of it as soon as you identify it. *But do not read it!*

2. *The material you may want to refer to later.* This is reference material. After you skim through it, you file it in some way, so that you can put your hand on it when you want it. You do *not* read it until you *must*.

3. *The material you want to understand thoroughly.* As you are sorting and skimming through written material, you run across a few things that you decide are *really* important to you. *This is the real reading.* Read this material carefully. Reread it, study it, and spend the time it takes to learn what is in it. Chances are very good indeed that the amount of material that comes to your desk that *must* be carefully read is far smaller than that in the two groups preceding.

There is probably another group of material that you may read for amusement or diversion. Detective stories are in this category, and so are the comics, magazine stories, and many novels. You may spoil these if you try too much system on them.

Rapid Reading

Your sorting process should cut down your required reading substantially. What is left may amount to less than 10 percent of all the reading material that comes your way. This figure does not mean much, of course, because it depends on the individual, his interests, and how critical he is.

Even with the material you are going to read, there is still some sorting to do. It pays to read summaries first. It pays to skim the material, reading only the beginning sentences of the paragraphs. It pays to look at pictures, diagrams, and figures. In approaching this material you are still doing so with critical caution. Could be you do not have to read it after all; perhaps the summary is all you need.

With the final sorting done, you can afford to practice reading the material rapidly. As you try this, remember that *you cannot acquire a skill all at once.* You have to keep trying.

The "trick" in rapid reading is to see and comprehend

more than a single word at a time. The more you can get at a glance, the faster you can read. With practice, you can eventually read a whole line at a time, or possibly more than that. Since many printed lines contain ten to fifteen words, what this means is that you may be able to read ten to fifteen times as fast if you are now a one-word-at-a-time reader.

One way to practice is to try to see and understand a phrase of several words at a quick glance. Look away from the page as soon as you have glanced at your group of words, and think about what you saw. When you have decided what the phrase meant to you, turn back and read each word of the phrase. Was your idea correct? If not, try again. If it was, try seeing a somewhat larger group of words. Try a whole line once in a while. In the end it will come to you, if you really want to learn badly enough to keep trying.

To many people, who are convinced that they simply cannot hope to read rapidly, all this may seem ridiculous. But great numbers of people have nevertheless become rapid readers through just this sort of process.[6] Progress may be— usually is—slow at first. But the ability to read and comprehend rapidly is worth a great deal in these times when we can learn so much from written material. It is possible, in many cities and in many government agencies, to get short courses in rapid reading. A supervisor really troubled by a slow reading habit may find it worthwhile to find out where he can get such a course.

The question really is, of course: What would it be worth to you to be able to read ten times as fast—or even twice as fast as you do now?

One last point needs to be made. This is that some material *must* be read slowly. Some people are able to read at a rate of six hundred to eight hundred words per minute, but they

6. A good article expanding this subject is Carol and Roger Bellows, "The Management of Learning," *Personnel Administration*, November–December 1960, pp. 19–26. "Speed Reading is the Bunk," by Eugene Ehrlich, may startle you. It was published in the *Saturday Evening Post*, June 9, 1962, pp. 10 and 16.

cannot do this accurately—with a textbook on mathematics or Lincoln's "Gettysburg Address." Thus the rate at which you read must be properly adapted to the material. You alone can judge this.

Every supervisor and his group of people are part of an *organization* of some kind. It may be small, perhaps consisting of only a few people. Or it may be large, consisting of hundreds, thousands, or even millions of people. It may be an organization of almost any kind—business, religious, governmental, industrial, medical, or some other. But whatever the kind or size, the organization, in one sense, is the house, the environment, the social system, the atmosphere, so to speak, in which the people work. For this reason, it is essential that a supervisor know something about organizations in general and a great deal about the organization of which he and his people are a part.

An organization is a group of people working together to get a job done. This job is often given different labels. Some call it the "objective," others call it the "goal" or "aim," and it is often called the "purpose." This "purpose" is the thing we get together to do—to build dams, manage national forests, manufacture radios, or collect taxes. In the case of the federal government, Congress usually states the purpose of an agency in what is called enabling legislation. The purpose of many business or industrial organizations is not always to be realized so readily.

Accomplishing the purpose of an organization is not simply a gang job. For example, in a dam-building organization not everyone works directly at the job of building dams. Some of the people design the dams, some buy the materials, some run machines, some hire laborers, some keep the books, and some do other kinds of jobs. All of these are essential to the principal purpose of building dams. What we are saying is that each of the people in an organization has a certain part of the job to do, a part that is important to the whole purpose. Obviously, there has to be someone to lead or head the organization who is responsible for seeing that the purpose is achieved, that everyone plays his proper part, and that the whole operation is well managed. This is the leader, chief, or administrator. The part he plays is of key importance to the work of the whole organization.

In a small organization it is possible for one man to perform many different tasks. In a larger organization these tasks may have to be divided up among a number of people, each doing a particular share of the job. And as organizations become large—still with a single purpose—a number of problems begin to appear that may seem unimportant in a small outfit. One of these problems is *coordination*. This is a broad term of many and often uncertain meanings. We use it here to mean *how we work together*, with everyone doing his part, and only his particular part, in such a way that we get the main job done as efficiently as possible and to the satisfaction of all concerned. This sounds simple enough, but coordination is often difficult to get.

Another problem of importance, especially in the big organizations, is the problem of communications. All of the people must be kept fully and currently informed of what is wanted and what is going on. Unless they are all able to work at their task with full understanding, the organization as a whole may not work at peak efficiency, and the purpose may not be correctly achieved. Large organizations sometimes employ specialists in communications to help solve this problem.

The Line-Staff Organization

There are many ways in which people and their tasks can be arranged in an organization in order to get work done efficiently. But most government agencies are organized in what is known as a line-staff system, and so are a good many businesses and industries. This system has been in use for many centuries, and credit is generally given to military organizations for developing it into an effective working tool. You may find in books on the subject a definition that reads something like this: The line-staff system is a chain of organization units operating under authority delegated from a central source; and at various points in the organization there are groups of people called staff, whose function is advisory as distinguished from the function of command.

This definition is correct, even if a little obscure. Let us then illustrate a simple line-staff organization thus:

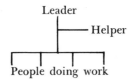

In this chart a leader is directing the work of four people. He has a man to help him do it. The helper is the leader's staff. The staff helper does no directing of the four people; he only helps the leader. Putting this another way: the leader has the responsibility for seeing that the organization gets its job done. He has the authority to see that it gets done properly. He has a staff officer to help him. The staff officer could be, say, a bookkeeper who keeps the accounts, pays the men, pays bills, and keeps track of profits or losses. The leader could probably do this himself, but we will assume he cannot look after everything and still get his main job done. So he has hired someone he can lean on, or depend on, to keep the books for him. In these words we have indicated where the word "staff" comes from, for a staff is a stick or pole you use to lean on. A staff, then, supports you, and in our chart the leader leans on the staff helper, who supports him or helps him by keeping the books.

About the time that the bookkeeper begins to feel that he should have more to say about running this little organization, trouble can develop. The leader may tell the workers to do one thing, but the bookkeeper tells them it would be better to do something else. The workers get confused; they become uncertain, and possibly do nothing at all. In this situation our staff helper has started giving orders, which is not what he was hired to do at all. Coordination is bad because not everyone is playing his proper part. Communications are bad, too, since there is misunderstanding as to what should be done. In order to get the organization humming again, the leader tells the bookkeeper *and* the four workers that he, and *only* he, will give the orders. The bookkeeper will give none; he will keep the accounts, pay the men, pay the bills, and keep track of profits and losses. When everyone understands, the group goes to work again. Thereafter the leader keep his eye on his overly ambitious staff helper and curbs any move on his part to assume command again.

Actually, of course, organizations are much more complex than this. But there is always a leader at the head of them: there are staff people who do special kinds of work; and there are workers who are doing the direct work on the main job. We can illustrate a more complex line-staff system like this:

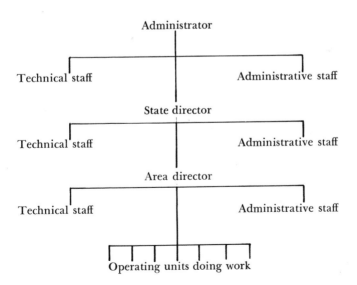

Administrator

Technical staff · · · · · · · · · Administrative staff

State director

Technical staff · · · · · · · · · Administrative staff

Area director

Technical staff · · · · · · · · · Administrative staff

Operating units doing work

In this chart, we can still see the leader. He goes by many names, depending on the organization; he may be called director, governor, chief, administrator, commissioner, superintendent, president, and so on. In this organization he has a technical staff consisting, let us say, of engineers. He also has an administrative staff; here the people deal with problems of budgeting, accounting, personnel, contracting, buying, selling, renting space, and other problems of similar character. The state director has similar but smaller staffs to help him with the technical and administrative problems in his state. The area director has a similar setup to help him deal with problems in his part of the state.

The main line in this line-staff organization runs from the administrator to the state director, to the area director, and finally to the operating units. This is what the military call the chain of command. This means simply that there is a chain, or line, of people in the organization who have the authority to give orders. The administrator gives orders to his state directors. None of his staff does this. In turn, the state director gives orders to his area directors, and again, the state staff people give no orders. The area director gives orders to the operating units under his direction and in his area. Here, again, the area staff issues no orders.

Here, then, as our definition said, we have a chain of organization units (national, state, and area), operating under authority given them or delegated from the administrator; and at various points (national, state, and area) there are groups of people called staff, whose function or duty is advisory, as distinguished from the function of command.

We should observe at this point that the state director, in order to operate successfully in his state, must have the authority. This authority is given to him by the administrator; that is, he is told that he has the authority to direct all the activities in his state. (His people are also told this.) In turn, the area director has to have the authority to direct work in his area. He gets this by delegation from the state director.

If either the state or area director could not act until they asked permission "up the line," the work would proceed pretty slowly. Thus, for large organizations, relatively extensive delegations of authority may be needed if the line people are to operate at full efficiency. In a very real sense, the state director *acts for* the administrator in the state. The area director does the same thing for the state director in his part (area) of the state.

In this larger organization (50 states, some 150 areas, and about 1,800 operating units) the same general rules are in effect—and the same kinds of problems occur—as in our very simple organization. Staff people who start giving orders cause confusion. Coordination and communications require special attention to keep the organization operating smoothly and efficiently.

Principles of Organization

We are now in a position to consider some principles or ideas that have been widely used to set up and run line-staff organizations.[1] These principles, if followed, will usually foster maximum efficiency and economy, involve the least confusion, and make the organization relatively easy to control. Also, coordination can be achieved reasonably well. What we are saying is that if you have an organization based on the following principles, the people who compose it will find it easier, more efficient, and less expensive to operate. We should note before we start that no matter how well organized a business or an agency may be, it cannot function at peak efficiency *unless the people in it use it properly.* With this proviso in mind, we may review the principles of organization as follows:

1. *Lines of authority in the organization must be clear.*

1. The reader is urged to review the book *It All Depends* by Harvey Sherman (University, Ala.: University of Alabama Press, 1966). The author calls this "a pragmatic approach to organization," meaning "doing what works in a given situation." The ideas expressed and discussed are highly useful to the practicing supervisor.

The lines of authority, or chains of command, must be well known to everyone in the organization. In the larger organization outlined above we have already noted the line running from the administrator to the state director, to the area director, to the operating units. There are, however, some other lines of authority that must be noted. For example, if there is a director of the administrative staff with, say, three divisions, each divided into several sections, there would be lines of authority between the heads of these groupings. We can chart this as follows:

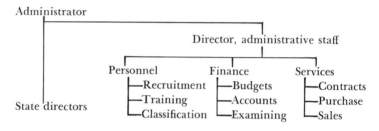

In this administrative staff group there is a line of authority from the director to the head of personnel, and thence to the sections on recruitment, training, and classification. There are similar lines through the finance division and the services division. You need not become confused on finding a "line" in a staff organization. The lines you see here are chains of command for just a segment of the total organization, that is, for the administrative staff group alone. This branch line does not conflict in any way with the main line from the administrator to his state directors, and on. The orders that flow over the branch line have largely to do with the administrative work of the various divisions.

As a corollary to our principle that lines of authority must be clear, it should also be noted that these channels of authority should not be violated by staff units. We have already seen the trouble that can develop even in a simple organization when staff people try to assume command. There is another problem of the same kind when a staff office in one location begins giving orders directly to a staff office in another place. For example, in the chart shown below, the orders having to do with personnel matters should go from the administrator to the state director.

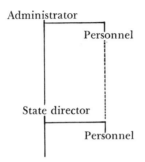

Orders should *not* flow from the director of the administrator's personnel staff to the director of the state director's personnel staff, as shown here by the dotted line. Orders should not flow between staff units *unless* the administrator has delegated authority for such action and everyone concerned understands the situation. Generally speaking, an administrator may safely permit routine and procedural matters to flow directly over the dotted line between the two staff divisions. But he is throwing the baby away with the bath if he permits his personnel staff to direct most or all of the personnel work in the organization. This is a serious error, since personnel matters are of key importance in any organization and, hence, of primary concern to line officers.

2. *Everyone in the organization should know* (a) *to whom he reports,* (b) *who reports to him; and no one should report to more than one supervisor.*

This is the principle of organization that is often called the "unity-of-command" principle. Any man who must report to two or three bosses is in for trouble. What does he do if he gets conflicting orders? Whose order does he carry out? And which order does he carry out first?

This principle of organization may seem so obvious and

so necessary that little emphasis needs to be placed on it. Even so, it is frequently violated, sometimes carelessly, sometimes unconsciously, by the very people who claim it to be obvious. We have already noted in our first principle of supervision that everyone should know who his supervisor is, and that he should have only one. Sometimes organization charts show what the correct situation should be, but in actual fact some people may have two supervisors and others none at all. A weak man in a supervisory job may sometimes let a stronger man in his group of people assume command. All this makes for confusion, inefficiency, and of course, poor morale.

3. *The responsibility and authority of each supervisor should be understood by everyone concerned.*

This principle applies, you will note, both to the supervisors and to the people they supervise. Everyone must understand in order that everyone can operate properly. The responsibility and authority are best expressed in writing, which is a fairly universal practice in the federal government but less so in industry. This helps to make the matter clear; but here again, activity in careless disregard of the principle can defeat even a clearly stated job description.

Let us note also that no individual or unit of an organization can be held responsible for the successful performance of any job unless the responsibility carries with it the authority to complete the job. Responsibility and authority must go hand in hand (see Principle 5, below).

4. *The number of people reporting to one supervisor should be no more than the number whose efforts he can effectively direct and coordinate.*

This is often called the principle of span of control. The idea is that if the span is too wide, the supervisor cannot give proper attention to each of his people. To understand the implications of this idea, we need to classify supervisors into two kinds: (a) those who supervise other supervisors, whom we shall call managers, and (b) those who supervise workers on a job, whom we shall call first-line supervisors.

The number of workers a first-line supervisor can have reporting to him depends on a great many things. He may be doing some work himself, other than supervision; in this case the number of people he can supervise depends in part on how much other work he is expected to do. This is a common enough situation in many organizations, but one we will not treat here, since it is a job mixture that has to be treated as an individual situation.

First-line supervisors who do nothing but supervise, ordinarily have from ten to twenty people reporting to them. The number depends on whether the group is all in one place or separated geographically. It depends also on how many new problems come up from day to day, and on how closely the work of one man interlocks with that of another. Where the people work together in one place, where all the people know quite well how to deal with the daily problems, and where there is very little overlapping of jobs, the supervisor can supervise the largest number of people. The more spread out the work is, or the closer the jobs interlock, or the more frequently new problems arise, the fewer people the supervisor can direct.

With respect to managers who supervise other supervisors, the situation is somewhat different. Even here, geographic spread, interlocking work, and new problems affect the number of supervisors that can report to one manager. But in addition, the work is entirely mental and may possibly demand more of a supervisor. As a matter of fact, there has been a great deal of argument about how many supervisors or executives one manager can direct. Many textbooks will tell you that the limit is five, and will refer you to the work of a man named Graicunas who "proved" this mathematically.[2] There seems nothing wrong with Graicunas' mathematics, but there are many who disagree with the assumptions on

2. See Lyndall F. Urwick, "The Manager's Span of Control," *Harvard Business Review*, May–June 1956, for a complete discussion of this.

which it is based. Other books will tell you that the idea of five is nonsense, and that there are plenty of well-managed corporations where the spans of control for managers run up to twenty-four or more.[3]

We may note here that the span of control in the government varies widely—as it does in business and industry. In some agencies four or five people commonly report to one manager; in others, as many as fifty report to one executive. In both situations the agencies may be well managed and successful. We can say, however, that an agency as well as a company is wise to study carefully the many factors affecting the span of control for its managers. The real question is: How does it work? The span should not be so wide that coordination and direction deteriorate, nor so narrow that the manager is literally "breathing down the necks" of his people. Careful testing and evaluation of results may have to be conducted over a long period to be sure the spans used are reasonably correct for each organizational situation.

5. *Authority to act should be delegated insofar as possible to the units or individuals nearest the point where the action must take place.*

The supervisor on the firing line usually knows better than anyone else what the problems are that he faces, and what needs to be done to overcome them. He has the best grasp of the conditions surrounding his work. He knows the people involved, he sees the need for action, and he urgently needs to take the action called for by the situation. To make him check "up the line" every time he wants to do something not only wastes his time but also wastes the time of the people up the line. They should not have to decide on every detail of action in every supervised unit.

Supervisors need authority to decide what to do and to act in the area of activity they are capable of judging locally. This authority should be delegated to them, and they should

3. This is discussed by W. W. Suojanen in "The Span of Control—Fact or Fable," *Advanced Management*, November 1955.

be held responsible for using it properly. To begin with, of course, the supervisors selected should have the ability to use necessary authority wisely.

6. *Every function needed to accomplish the organization's purpose should be assigned to a unit of the organization.*

It seems obvious that all the jobs to be done should be assigned to one unit or another of the organization. It is not unusual to find, however, that some particular job has been left hanging in the air and that confusion results when several units try to take care of it at the same time. Here we need again to note that functions assigned to units should be clear, specific, and easily understood. It goes almost without saying that all this should be in writing. This is one of the reasons for organization charts.

7. *The organization should be as simple as possible.*

The idea applies especially to the number of so-called levels. For example, in the following chart, organization B appears simpler than organization A.

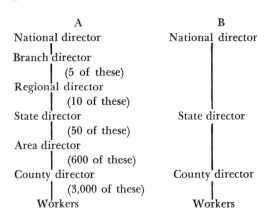

                    A   B
            National director   National director
            Branch director
                   (5 of these)
            Regional director
                   (10 of these)
            State director   State director
                   (50 of these)
            Area director
                   (600 of these)
            County director   County director
                   (3,000 of these)
            Workers   Workers

In this example, working in organization A will generally be more difficult than in B. Orders from the national director will take longer to reach the sixth level in the county than in B where it is the third level. Information will take longer to go either up or down the line, and there are more places where the orders may be "interpreted," that is, changed. In A the county director, tired of waiting for urgently needed decisions, may make an "end run"—that is, if he can get away with it, he will try to reach the regional or the national director without going through all the directors in between. This by-passing of levels will cause confusion, and there are many examples of it to be found in organizations with too many levels. We cannot put all the blame for the end runs on the county director; a simpler organization would remove the temptation and the necessity.

We must note that while organization B is simpler with respects to levels, the directors in it necessarily have a much wider span of control than those in A. In A the span of control for any director is 5, except for the state director, who has 12. In B the span of control is 50 for the national director and 50 to a 100 or more for the state director. A simple device for cutting down these latter spans, which are too wide, is to divide very large states into two or three areas, each with a director. Smaller states need not be so divided. This introduces an additional level in organization B, but only to a limited extent, and only for special situations.

There are many ways in which organizations can get too complex. Too many small staff units at each level, instead of a few combined, larger ones, can slow down staff operation. Too many assistants, each with a small segment of work to watch over, can slow down the work. Mixed-up staff units at different levels can cause trouble; for example, if payrolls are prepared by a financial staff at one level, but by a personnel staff at another level, then coordination becomes more difficult.

All such examples—and there are many more—lead us to the need for constant review of any organization structure. Just because an organization has always been organized in a particular way is no reason why it should keep on in the same way indefinitely. Both in industry and in government, "organizational paralysis" has led to disaster often enough. The need for change leads us finally to our last principle, which is:

8. *An organization should be flexible, but ordinarily changes in it should be made gradually except under highly special conditions.*

It is one thing for an organization to be flexible, but quite another for it to be shaken or rocked by administrative earthquakes. In the government, for example, possibly as much waste of money has resulted from large-scale reorganizations as from any other action. New administrators, especially those of limited experience, are often prone to move too quickly in reorganizing an agency. Instead of studying their agency carefully, then changing the organization structure gradually, they move on the basis of preconception to bring about a good "shake-up." The moment word gets out—which it does with great speed regardless (or even because) of secrecy —the wildest rumors streak through the agency. People gather in small groups to speculate about the impending changes. Work, except routine stuff, comes almost to a standstill. Many people leave for jobs elsewhere. The rest wait to see what is going to happen—a very natural reaction to any kind of impending change. The deterioration of a formerly smoothly operating agency and the consequent loss in productive output are tremendous and unnecessary.

In contrast, an experienced administrator works with the people on his staff and, indeed, with his whole organization, on the new objectives that should be reached. Once these are clear, he begins making small moves to reform his organization, so that it can most easily reach these objectives. Reorganization goes on all the time, but always aimed at objectives the whole organization understands. Implicit in this more gradual approach is the realization that organizations are made up of *people,* and that trained, experienced people are the greatest asset an organization has. It is not change that hurts an organization, but rather failure on the part of the leaders of an organization to supply its people with timely information about the change.

Some Ideas on Staff Work

Before we leave our consideration of organization, it may be worthwhile to add a final note on the operation of staff people. Somehow, in many organizations, staff personnel begin to feel they are not really playing a proper part in the program going on. Their advice may not be taken; they may not even be asked for it. Administrators may make decisions without reference to their staff specialists; indeed, they may become impatient with the kind of staff advice they receive. Sometimes this failure results in quite serious consequences. And there may be a great many reasons why staff and line people are unable to work together.

Some years ago an idea was widely circulated in the Department of Defense and, since then, elsewhere in the government service. The idea seems to have come originally from an official paper by Major General Archer L. Learch. It had to do with what is called completed staff work. The suggestions apply both to the line officer and to the staff officer. They are shown in the chart.

Some Conclusions

We are now in a position to state a few general conclusions about organizations that supervisors may want to keep in mind, as follows:

1. While every supervisor scarcely needs to be an expert on organization theory, he does need to be fully familiar with the organization of which he and his people are a part. He ought to be able to draw a chart of his agency, showing its line and staff units and what each does and is responsible for. Obviously, he should know who the people are who man the various units of his outfit, most especially those who may deal fairly closely with the work of his group.

2. Every supervisor should be familiar with the principles of organization, such as those we have discussed in this chap-

COMPLETED STAFF WORK

How to Get It

Assign the problem and request its solution in such a way that completed staff work is readily possible.

1. Know the problem.

2. Make one individual responsible to you for the solution.

3. State the problem to him clearly, precisely; explain reasons, background; limit the area to be studied.

4. Give the individual the advantage of your knowledge and experience in this problem.

5. Set a time limit; or request assignee to estimate completion date.

6. Assure him that you are available for discussion as work progresses.

If you were the subordinate, would *you* consider the guidance, given at the time the assignment is made and as the directed work progresses, to be adequate for readily completed staff work? Adequate guidance eliminates wasted effort and makes for completed staff work.

How to Do It

Study the problem and present its solution in such form that only approval or disapproval of the completed action is required.

1. Work out all details completely.

2. Consult other staff officers.

3. Study, write; restudy, rewrite.

4. Present a single, coordinated, proposed action. Do not equivocate.

5. Do not present long memoranda or explanations. Correct solutions are usually recognizable.

6. Advise the chief what to do. Do not ask him.

If you were the chief, would *you* sign the paper you have prepared and thus stake your professional reputation on its being right? If not, take it back and work it over, it is not yet completed staff work.

—*From the U.S. Department of Defense*

ter. These principles may be stated in different ways, but the ideas they express have stood up pretty well for many centuries. Almost certainly, better principles will be found as we learn more about how to work together. In the meantime, it behooves supervisors to know the best there is to know, so that they may contribute intelligently to the improvement of their own organization. It' is possible that some supervisors will be called upon sooner or later to help reorganize or to set up an agency or a unit of one. It would be well if they were prepared.

3. Obviously, organization structure is important only in relation to the people composing it. Supervisors should remember that no organization, no matter how perfect, can survive and succeed unless the people within it work together for its survival and success.

4. The people in an organization must never lose sight of the objective or purpose of their organization. In a large, far-flung organization this is not always an easy thing to do, but its objective is the key to all the work it does.

5. Communications within an organization must always be kept in top operating condition. Any time the people come to feel that they do not know and understand what is going on, the work of the organization is in danger of falling off. If the communications become bad enough, an organization may eventually segment itself into a mass of fragments subsisting largely on the grapevine.

6. What may be called the "administrative climate" of an organization, needs to be a good one. The management and supervisory people are the ones who generate the climate. It should be one in which no man is afraid to speak his mind or fearful of reprisals if he indulges in some original thinking. It should be such that people enjoy working in it, enjoy their work, and take pride in their organization. The idea applies equally to the organization as a whole and to each small supervisory unit within it.[4]

4. See also Likert's "System 4" type of organization, described on page 85.

7. And finally, in summary, it is of key importance that managers and supervisors of the organization understand that the most valuable asset is its people. It is never in the interest of good administration to sacrifice people to organizational changes or arrangements. No organizational theory can long survive that is in conflict with sound principles of human behavior and human relations.[5]

5. To understand fully all that may be involved in items 3, 6, and 7 above, the serious student may find it useful to study *Integrating the Individual and the Organization* by Chris Argyris (New York: John Wiley & Sons, 1964).

11   Some Management Activities

So far, we have been giving most of our attention to the ways in which supervisors and their people can work together. We have done this because every supervisor is concerned with ideas such as these. But other kinds of activities are also essential to the work of a unit of organization. These are different in character from the strictly human relationships, and they have much to do with the way in which the unit functions. For our purposes we may call them management activities, although we must note that "management" is a word of many meanings. (Sometimes "management" is used to mean both supervision and the direction of operating systems. It is also used to denote the directing group of an organization. This group is often called "top management" or simply, "management.")

Management, as we use the word here, depends on the size and kind of organization segment headed by a supervisor. All supervisors must perform some of these management activities, but some supervisors deal with more than others. For example, every supervisor needs to plan and schedule work, but not every supervisor must develop financial plans (that is, budgets), since not all supervisors are concerned with the management of funds. Similarly, not all supervisors manage communication systems, although every supervisor needs to be skilled in communicating with the people in his unit.

In this chapter we consider some ideas about work loads, planning, scheduling, and the efficiency with which work is done. Such things as these are matters concerning every supervisor, not just a few in "top management."

Work Loads

The amount of work a supervisor and his people must do each day, or week, or month, or year is commonly spoken of as their work load. This is something in which all of us are considerably interested. Usually the work load varies in some way from period to period, alternately reaching high and low points, depending on the kind of work being done. Supervisors have to make whatever advance arrangements they can to be sure their people are not overloaded part of the time and only partly occupied the rest of the time. More than this, the load must be fairly shared by all the people in the unit. No one should have to carry more—or less—than his fair share, and importantly also, the various kinds of work should be correctly assigned to the proper people. This helps to avoid using high-priced people to do low-priced work, or the reverse.

In any event, there is a simple way to study or review work loads in relation to people that will help a supervisor considerably in dealing with these problems. The method is often called work-load analysis. We make such an analysis to find out:

1. What the various jobs are that make up the work load.
2. How many jobs of each kind there are to do.
3. About how long it will take to do each kind of job.
4. Who can best do each kind of job, in terms of kinds and grades or salaries of personnel.

Once we have the facts about each one of these four items clearly set forth, we are in a position to judge whether our unit is correctly staffed, whether the work is correctly assigned and shared, and what steps might be necessary to correct any unbalanced situation that may come to light.

The first thing we have to do is to state as precisely as we can what the work load is for a given period of time. For certain kinds of work we might do this on a daily basis. For example, in a janitor job, there may be a hundred rooms and forty thousand square feet of hallways to be cleaned each night. Or for a typist pool, there may be an average of three hundred pages a day to be typed. However, we would not use a daily rate for a group of lawyers who might be expected to prepare two hundred briefs each year. Thus a supervisor needs to select for review a period of time that has most meaning for his particular kind of work. These periods are affected by all sorts of conditions, such as climate (for agricultural workers), pay periods (for payroll units), weather (for janitor groups), congressional sessions (for budget groups), court sessions (for lawyers), and so on.

We might note, in passing, some symptoms that may indicate the need for a work-load study. An obvious one is the apparent need for continuous overtime work. Another is a backlog of some kind that never seems to get done. Another is that Joe always seems to have more than he can do while Susie never seems to keep busy. Still another is that no one ever seems to make use of some of the work turned out, and there is doubt as to whether it really needs to keep on being done. And so on. Usually it is not enough to try to deal directly with such symptoms. They indicate that something is out of adjustment; the question is, what?

Almost always, as we go ahead to make a work-load analysis, we find that the total load of work is made up of a group or series of jobs. For example, in the janitor job mentioned above, the force may actually have to do a variety of things, such as:

Sweep 100 rooms.

Wash 40,000 square feet of hallways.

Vacuum-clean 40 rugs.

Empty 120 wastebaskets.

Dust desks, tables, chairs, and files in 100 rooms.

Collect soap, brooms, cleaners, and other supplies from supply room and haul to area. Return these at end of job.

This breakdown into a series of jobs is usually possible for

all but the simplest work loads. Such a breakdown should
consist of jobs or groups of jobs that are performed more or
less as units. We do this in order to be able to say about how
long each unit ought to take. In our janitor example, experience may have shown that it takes about 12 minutes to sweep
a room, about 20 minutes to vacuum a rug, and so on. On
such a basis, we can then say that it will require 1,200 minutes, or 20 hours, to sweep 100 rooms, and 800 minutes, or
13 hours, to vacuum 40 rugs. All these data begin to get a
little cumbersome itemized this way, so we organize them on a
simple sheet like this:

Kind of Job	Number	Rate	TOTAL TIME REQUIRED (hours)
Sweep rooms	100	12 min.	1,200 min. = 20
Vacuum rugs	40	20 min.	800 min. = 13
Dust furniture in	100	15 min.	1,500 min. = 25
rooms			
Wash hallway floors	40,000	1 hr./	= 40
(sq. ft.)		1,000 sq. ft.	
Empty wastebaskets	120	5 min.	600 min. = 10

As we list the kinds of jobs, their number, and the rate at
which each one can be done, we are able then to see the time
needed to take care of each part of the work load and, finally,
the total time required for all of it.

This analysis still does not tell us what kinds of people
should be doing each job. Let us suppose, for the sake of
example, that we can use grade-one people to dust, sweep,
and empty wastebaskets, but that we need grade-three people
to handle the machines used for vacuuming rugs and wash-
ing floors. Our analysis form will need a little expansion as
shown on the following page.

Thus far our analysis seems to show the need for about
seven people in grade one and very close to seven in grade
three. (We get this by dividing the totals by eight hours.)
But this is not all there is to it. There are a number of inci-

Kind of Job	Number	Rate	TIME REQUIRED (hours)		
			Grade 1	Grade 3	Total
Sweep rooms	100	12 min.	20		20
Vacuum rugs	40	20 min.		13	13
Dust furniture in rooms	100	15 min.	25		25
Wash hallway floors (sq. ft.)	40,000	1 hr./ 1,000 sq. ft.		40	40
Empty wastebaskets	120	5 min.	10		10
Total			55	53	108

dental jobs that are sure to come up—something spilled on a rug takes special cleaning; a cracked desk glass needs reporting; a number of light bulbs need changing, etc. All these, if handled by the same force, take time too and must be allowed for on some kind of basis.

Last, note that if there is need for 108 man-hours of work per night, then this cannot be done by 14 people unless this is *all* they do. Coffee breaks, special jobs, staff meetings, sick and annual leave, and the like take time and must be counted. Also, of course, someone is needed to supervise the entire operation. His work does not include sweeping, dusting, and other such services, but rather checking, training, guiding, evaluating production, making work-load studies, and the like—that is, *supervising*.

In making a work-load analysis, a supervisor will do well to keep such points as the following in mind:

1. The list of jobs to be done should not be too detailed. If the work is broken into a long series of very small parts, the analysis is likely to become bogged down in the mass of details. In our janitor example, we could have shown the exact number of chairs, large tables, small tables, file cases, telephone stands, etc., necessary to be dusted, with a rate for each one. But from a practical standpoint, a supervisor can afford to group them all into one item of "furniture per room," since he knows pretty well what each room will con-

tain. The point here is that we make a work-load analysis to help us get a job done, not just for the sake of an elaborate study itself. Being too elaborate about such a study is characteristic of inexperienced supervisors.

2. The rates, that is, the average time per job unit, have to be set with reasonable accuracy. There are a number of ways of finding out what they are. One is to check a number of people as they work to find out what a good average rate is. Another is to divide the total time it takes to do a large number of such jobs by the number completed. Results from these two methods can be compared to see how well they coincide.

The impulse is often almost overwhelming to cut the rates down. It may appear that if everyone worked just a little harder, considerably more work could be accomplished. But the catch is in whether everyone is going to "work a little harder." Here, a supervisor will do well to remember the difference between a driver and a leader, and to recollect that participation of his people in making such analyses may often provide many new ways of dealing with the situation. People who are proud of their outfit will be quite ingenious in suggesting ways to improve rates—and in carrying them out. People who are resentful at being handed rates they disagree with are quite unlikely to reach them, except under heavy prodding, with consequent ill feeling and with slowdowns the moment pressure is relaxed.

3. Distributing work among various kinds and grades of personnel requires a supervisor to know a little about job classification. In our janitor example, the distinction is between only two kinds, but a great many kinds may be required for more complex work. In the engineering work of the government service, for example, there are nine grades of engineering technicians. In what grade of work is each job? Or in many kinds of professional work, as many as eighteen grades may be available to choose from.

Note that we cannot afford to select the grade and kind of

personnel simply on the basis of what has always been done before. This needs rechecking and reevaluating from time to time, especially as either the work or the classification standards may change. If we are wrong in our classification of personnel and grades, our whole analysis becomes far less useful.

Drawing Conclusions

Once we have completed a work-load analysis, and are satisfied that the picture it portrays is reasonably accurate, we begin to consider what we need to do about the findings. Three general items may show up:

1. We may find that we have the wrong kind of people doing certain jobs. This may seem a little silly, but it is quite common. It often occurs that skilled people devote part or most of their time to unskilled work. Since skilled people command higher pay, the work then costs more than it should. If unskilled people are performing a lot of skilled work, either their work is not as good as it should be; or there is doubt whether the work really calls for skill; or the unskilled people possibly have become skilled and should be reclassified.

It is common enough also to find people doing the wrong kind of work in areas where a distinction is made between professional and subprofessional work. What kind of work is professional? How much subprofessional work should a professional man do? The two kinds of work are often very closely associated and hard to separate. Ambitious subprofessional people may often try to do more of the professional work, possibly, than they should. What guides do we use here?

It is well to keep in mind that professional and skilled workers are more highly paid than subprofessional or unskilled. Thus people who are professional or skilled will cost more, and their efforts should be directed to the kind of work for which they are best fitted. It is also well for government supervisors to keep in mind precisely stated classification standards and specifications for jobs in the government service. These—with the help of a classification analyst—can be of real use to a supervisor faced with problems of this kind.

2. We may find that some of our people are in the wrong grade, that is, they are being paid either too much or too little for the kind of work they are doing. Either situation presents a problem that should be dealt with promptly, since either situation means an injustice is being done to someone. Because position grades must be set with due regard for classification standards and specifications, here again the supervisor may wish to consult a classification specialist for help.

3. We may find that we have too many, or too few, people in total, or that we have too many of one kind of personnel and too few of another. In any case, the supervisor needs to plan on making such adjustments as seem called for. In this case, one's own supervisor should be consulted and, in the end, the personnel office.

4. We may find—or know already—that the work load fluctuates, hitting a high point, every so often, that the regular working group simply cannot handle. There are two ways to deal with this:

a. We may ask members of the unit to work overtime for short periods in order to meet the deadlines involved.

b. We may employ additional people on a temporary basis to help tide over the high period.

Planning and Scheduling

No supervisor can do much of a job unless he has clearly in mind what he intends to do the next day, next week, next month, and next year. Some kinds of work call for looking farther ahead than others. But every kind requires that careful thought be given to what should be done in the future. The business of deciding ahead of time what we will do when the time comes is generally spoken of as planning. A good supervisor must, without question, also be a good planner.

A plan of work can be set up conveniently for about a year ahead. This is not too long a time to be impractical, nor so short as to keep us constantly developing new plans. For some supervisors, two, three, or five years may be better. Others may want to plan no more than a few months ahead. And indeed, there are no rules for this. One uses the period of time best suited to the work being done. But whatever period is chosen, a simple way to proceed is as follows:

1. We look ahead over the period and think of the important jobs we hope to get done. As we do this, we consider the resources we have, in manpower, materials, supplies, equipment, and other items. We write down all the things we hope to accomplish in a simple list. To start with, we do not have to worry about which comes first; we can arrange the items later. And we write until we cannot think of any more subjects; if we find that we have omitted some, we add them. It is not necessary to describe each item in detail: each one should be just explicit enough to call to mind what is intended.

2. The items are rearranged in some sort of order. Most supervisors find that they cannot accomplish everything they would like to in a single year—especially in view of available resources and staff. So first things are put first. Items on the tail end of the list may not get done—or they may, if everything works out as the supervisor hopes.

3. Next, the items can be expanded a little, important details added, special phases given special attention.

4. Following this, something needs to be put down indicating *how* the job can best be done.

5. Next we can show *who* is going to do each job, that is, which people or person will be assigned to which item.

6. Finally, we begin to set some sort of timetable for getting things done. This leads us into *scheduling*.

It is obvious that material such as the foregoing may conveniently be arranged in some uniform manner, for example, on a columnar pad with headings something like these:

Job or Activity	How	Who	When Where (if necessary)
A numbered list of the things we plan on doing	Here we set forth the way we will do the things we plan	The people assigned to each job or activity	In these columns we can indicate when and where the work is to be done

Another useful format might be this:

Job	January	February	March	April	etc.
1.	In these columns Who, How, and Where				
2.	are listed for each item.				
3.					

The list and format above are merely suggestive. There are all sorts of ways to develop a plan and to put it in usable form. All of them must rely on a clear conception on the part of the planner as to what he wants to do. No format, no written list, has any greater value than the thinking one does about the future needs and work.

Scheduling

Some supervisors prefer to combine their timetable with their plans. Others prefer to develop a plan that contains only deadline dates for completion of an item, or only general indications of the period when the work will be performed. Whether timetables or schedules are prepared as part of a plan or separately, however, *they had better be prepared*. Various studies have shown that there is a high degree of correlation between good scheduling and high productivity. Putting this another way, well-scheduled work is likely to get done in a more orderly way and at less cost.

Some ideas about scheduling that have proved valuable are these:

1. If you try to make only a single schedule for a long period ahead, you may discover that it is impossible to be precise about things many months ahead. For this reason it may be better to develop two kinds of schedules rather than only one. The first is a long-term schedule, say for a full year ahead. In this schedule the timing is somewhat general in character, as for example, "spring," "fall," "late August," and the like. Specific dates are put in the long-term schedule only when they are certainly known far ahead of time.

The second schedule is a short-term one, used to cover a period from one to several weeks ahead. Actually this is the immediate portion of a long-term schedule crystallized for specific action. In this one we can get specific not only on days, but also on the time of day, if we like.

2. Schedules should be developed steadily. As the year rolls along, you can add items and general dates on the far end of the long-term schedule, while the nearer portions are eaten up by the short-term schedule. The short-term schedule must be prepared at short intervals of a week or two, or ahead of whatever other interval you may be using.

3. Schedule everything to be done, insofar as practical. Obviously, despite the most careful scheduling, unexpected matters will come up that will strain or break your schedule. Even so, this is not a valid reason for neglecting to schedule all jobs and activities. The more fully you can organize your work into a schedule, the nearer you can come to peak efficiency.

4. Hold to your schedule as closely as practical. It is, of course, foolish to adhere blindly to a schedule just because it has been set. You should run the schedule; do not let it run you. But again, the closer you can come to your schedule,

the better for your work. Never deviate from it without good reason.

5. Plan for the unexpected. Since everyone knows that unexpected matters will come up from time to time, it is wise to provide for them in your schedule. At judicious intervals your schedule ought to have openings in it for the nonscheduled matters. This allows for emergency adjustment. It is another way of saying that too tight a schedule often comes to grief.

6. Coordinate your schedule with those of people who work with you. It is obviously preferable to do this ahead of time, rather than be forced to change your timetable on short notice.

7. Keep your schedule showing. It is very important that the people with whom you work know that you have a schedule and that you stick to it rather closely. People will not respect your schedule if they do not know you have one. Posting a schedule on the wall or bulletin board is generally a good thing to do in any office. Review it frequently.

8. Analyze completed schedules from time to time to see if you could have prepared a better one in the light of the way things finally worked out. You may discover that you have a habit of scheduling too tightly or too loosely, of omitting things, of abandoning your schedule when you should have stuck to it, etc. A critical review of finished schedules will often provide you with ideas for making better ones. Experience is indeed a great teacher, if you use it.

Besides these suggested ideas, it is worth noting that schedules cannot plan and organize work. Their value is in setting forth plans on a time basis; usefulness in this respect is no greater than the excellence of the planning that must precede its use. Furthermore, the supervisor who lets his schedule control him, instead of controlling his schedule, is in for trouble. A schedule must be as flexible as possible. A rigid one can easily destroy the value of the planning.

Making Work-Improvement Studies

Anyone trying to do a job usually finds he can best get it done in a number of steps. A little job may take only a few steps. A big job may take many. The series of steps to get the job done is usually called a procedure. Obviously, a short procedure containing a few steps is preferable to a long one containing many—provided the short procedure gets the job done just as well.

Job procedures may be called job methods or techniques, but by whatever name they are known, there is a tendency for them to grow. When many people are involved in the doing of a job, and everyone tries to get in on the act, it is inevitable that more steps begin to creep into the procedure used for getting it done.

Procedures are what they are not only because there are jobs to be done, but also because:

1. There is a law.
2. There is a regulation.
3. There is a policy.

In addition, there are other factors affecting procedures, including:

4. Custom.
5. Work habits.
6. Misunderstanding of policy (i.e., our "interpretation").

All these things can so modify a procedure as to change it from a simple set of steps to a complex grouping of many steps. All six factors tend to make a procedure longer. Worse, they tend to stifle initiative, stultify good judgment, increase costs, lengthen the time it takes to get the job done, and make work much harder than it need be.

When a procedure gets cumbersome enough, we say that it is "all fouled up in red tape." What we usually mean when we say this is that rules and regulations make it virtually impossible to operate without exasperating delay and a great many procedural steps. We do not usually mean that *we* cause the red tape, that is, that *our* work habits, or *our* customs, or *our* misunderstanding of policy, is creating the red tape.

The fact is, however, that any one or all of the six factors may operate to lengthen or complicate our procedures. The unfortunate part about it is that the factors operate insidiously. Little by little, the procedure gets a little longer. One step is added, then another, each one most thoroughly justified! Until at length we find ourselves wound up in red tape without quite knowing how it happened.

Let it be noted that procedures full of a great many steps tend to be characteristic of any big organization—government, business, industrial, or other. We cannot blindly assume that we have no such thing in *our* particular organization. The six factors operate in every organization.

Once we can honestly recognize that this sort of thing can happen here, then the problem of what to do about it is on the way to being solved. What we need to do from time to time is to review critically *all* our job procedures or methods to find out whether they are indeed the best we know. We need to find out whether *all* the steps are necessary, or only some; whether the steps follow one another in the right order and place; whether the procedure can be shortened, so as to make the job easier; or indeed, whether the procedure is necessary at all.

These reviews of the steps we take—the procedure we use —in getting a job done, we call work-improvement studies. In making such a study we need to answer the question: Is there a simpler, easier, faster, less expensive way to do this job and still get the results we want?

This question cannot be answered by saying that the law requires it, or that it is a company or agency policy. If it is clear that there is indeed a better way to do the job, were it not for laws, rules, or policy, then it is only common sense to question the validity of these impeding factors. Laws and regulations as well as policies are made by people, and they can be changed if there are sound reasons for doing so. It does not always follow that they *ought* to be changed, because there may be good reasons for them other than the way they affect job procedures. Nevertheless, *they can be changed,* and anyone making work-improvement studies must keep this in mind.

To illustrate how one might make a work-improvement study, let us consider the following simple case. If it seems somewhat ridiculous, let it be noted that red tape often looks that way to people who are not involved.

A few years ago, on a college campus, I ran across this situation. A truck had delivered a big pile of sand to the edge of a road. A workman was hauling the sand in a wheelbarrow across the lawn to a large bed of flowers and shrubs. There he spread the sand on the soil, presumably to loosen it.

The workman stopped the wheelbarrow ten feet away from the pile of sand, took the shovel, walked over to the sand pile, took a shovelful of sand, walked back to the wheelbarrow, and dumped the sand in it. He did this until the wheelbarrow was full. Then he turned the wheelbarrow around and wheeled it over to the flower bed. There he spread the sand on top of the ground.

Almost everyone is amused at such a workman. Two very obvious improvements he ought to make are:

1. He ought to place the wheelbarrow alongside the sand, so he could shovel without walking back and forth.

2. He ought to head it toward the flower bed before he fills it, since it is easier to turn an empty barrow than a full one.

Usually people also ask, "Why didn't the truck dump the sand at the edge of the flower bed in the first place, instead of at the edge of the road?" The answer is that the college's policy was to keep trucks off the fine lawn. Presumably, therefore, in this simple situation, about all we can do is carry out the two improvements we have already suggested, unless the college authorities agree to change their rule.

But before we give up, do any other questions occur to you? The key question here—as in all such studies—is *why?* This was the question that solved the whole problem: *Why* put sand on the flower bed? Answer: Well, it's supposed to loosen the soil. Question: Does it? Answer: No, not on this particular soil, and not as well as lime. Only a little lime would be needed, not a big pile as of the sand. As it turned out, a hundred-pound sack of lime did the job, in one trip of the wheel barrow.

The point, of course, in this deceivingly simple situation, is that you *never take anything for granted.* Not until the necessity for the whole process was questioned did it turn out that practically all of it could be eliminated.

In making a critical and objective appraisal of any procedure, we are quite likely to encounter an apparently valid reason for what seems to be a foolish or unnecessary step. It is important that the reason be subjected to scrutiny and properly identified. If the reason is a law or policy, then consideration needs to be given to the advisability of changing it. If the reason is rooted in our customs or habits, we need to consider how we may change these. Frequently enough, the reason for a foolish step is found to be our own misunderstanding or misinterpretation of a rule, rather than the rule itself. Because this is so, we can never safely assume we know what the rule is until we carefully recheck it.

In summary, let me note that no one should undertake a work-improvement study unless he is prepared to take the consequences. Commonly, such studies result, or should result, in changes. If changes make you uncomfortable, do not make the study. The interesting thing about these studies is that you can operate without restriction in making them. For purposes of the study you can—indeed you must—question laws, rules, policies, regulations, customs, etc. No cow is too sacred. The paramount question is to find a better way to do a job. In the end, possibly the future of the organization lies in how skillfully and systematically we make our work-improvement studies.

THE PEOPLE TO MAKE THE STUDY

By far the best way to make a work-improvement study is with the group of people who are most familiar with the procedure to be examined, that is, who regularly use the procedure. This is so for two very important reasons:

1. These people know more about the procedure than anyone else. It is their job. Their statements are therefore most likely to be factually correct and the least theoretical.

2. These same people are the ones who will be affected if the procedure is changed. If *they* help change it, they will accept the change readily enough, since it is their own doing. If someone else develops the change, and tries to get them to adopt it, they are likely to find all sorts of reasons why it cannot be used. Since these people are the ones who use the procedure, they can and do nullify attempts to change it unless there is a rigorous (and expensive) policing of the new method. With an eye to the future, therefore, enlist the efforts of the people to be affected by any change. This is the easiest way to gain acceptance.

Even so, it is advisable for at least a few members of the study group to be unfamiliar with the procedure because:

a. People completely familiar with a procedure tend to accept the steps in it without question.

b. People strange to the procedure, or armed with no more than a general knowledge of it, tend to question everything about it, or at least to be more critical.

In general, the chairman of the study group had best be someone a step removed from the users of the procedure, but who has a reasonably good knowledge of the subject. Furthermore, the chairman has to be a skilled conference leader, able to draw ideas out of the group without submerging them in his own. He needs to be able to stimulate objectivity and skepticism. He must be intolerant of sloppy thinking and quick to detect too ready or too tacit acceptance of invalid reasons for procedural steps. The chairman's job is fun, but it calls for quick thinking. Indeed, studies of job procedures are usually fun for everyone. After all, there are no hampering laws or policies that control the making of them.

The climate for work-improvement studies has to be congenial, too. Everyone knows that tomatoes will not ripen in a dank, cold climate. They must have sun. And in making a work-improvement study, the climate has to be conducive to the operation of free intelligence and good common sense. A skillful chairman sets the stage carefully. He convinces the people that they are there to try to make their job easier, that their ideas are really wanted, that they can safely question the most sacred of policies, and that mutiny, so to speak, is a good thing. The people are encouraged to ask "Why?" about every procedural detail. If at any time the chairman by his attitude seems to the participants to be censoring or condemning their ideas, the climate will become dank and cold, and new ideas are most unlikely to ripen thereafter.

THE STEPS IN A WORK-IMPROVEMENT STUDY

A simple and practical procedure for making a work-improvement study (it, too, is a job) involves five steps, as follows:

1. Set forth clearly what the job is supposed to accomplish. This is the objective, and it acts as the standard to check against.

2. List each step in the procedure used to do the job and number it. Be sure to put in *all* the details; they have a habit of becoming important. And be sure that each step is *correctly* described.

3. Question each step in order, after they have all been listed. The whole group does this. They ask such questions as these: *Why* is it necessary? *What* purpose does it serve? Is this the best *place* to do it? The best *time?* The best *person* to do it? Isn't there a *better way* to do the step? And so on.

4. Develop a new procedure. This results rather easily from steps 2 and 3 above. All unnecessary steps are cut out, all possible details eliminated, all possible combinations of steps are made, better steps inserted, and the series is rearranged to be in the best possible order. All this is done regardless of law, policy, regulation, or what has customarily been done in the past. For future reference, we make a note of any such things that act to prevent the improvements.

5. The new procedure is either put into use as soon as practical, or if policy or regulation stand in the way, approval is sought for a change in them. If the policy or regulation can be changed by the proper authority, then the new procedure goes into effect.

An additional step ought to be put in this study procedure. This is to *evaluate* the new procedure. When steps are eliminated, it is usually possible to find out how much time is saved, how many forms are eliminated, how much filing is made unnecessary, and so on. All these things cost money. An hour a day at $2 an hour adds up to an annual cost reduction of $520. Filing space is worth several dollars per square foot. And so on. If it is necessary to get a policy or rule changed in order to install a new procedure, dollar costs provide useful arguments. Thus, between steps 4 and 5 above, we may need this evaluation step. We may also find it useful to check our estimates against actual costs *after* the new procedure is put into effect—just to be sure our new procedure really saves time and money.

When a Work-Improvement Study Is Needed

Many supervisors who have never undertaken such studies as these are often uncertain where and how to begin. If you feel this way, scan the following list. If any of these conditions are true in your unit, why not do a study to see if things can be made easier?

1. Too much paperwork.

2. Too much red tape.

3. Too many copies required of this or that form or report, or too many forms or reports.

4. Too many mistakes being made.

5. Procedures too cumbersome.

6. Some operations seem to take more time than they should.

7. Costs too high.

8. Too much waste.

9. A bottleneck slowing things down.

It is seldom that a supervisor can say none of these things are true of his unit. If you feel this way, better ask your people. They may have a different idea.

Experience in many organizations shows clearly that no matter how efficient a procedure may seem, you had better re-study it after no more than three years. Procedures tend to get more complex. Furthermore, times change and so do people. Enough change takes place in three years to warrant review of any procedure. If your procedures have not been studied for five years, chances are they can be much improved.

Experienced supervisors have found that devoting a few hours of their entire group's time to such studies regularly, once a month, can pay dividends. If, say, on the first Monday (or any other day that suits), everyone stops regular work and goes at a work-improvement study, there is hope for greater efficiency. This also enables all the people to participate— and as we have already seen, this pays.

12   *Solving Problem Cases*

If every supervisor started his unit from the beginning, and did a topnotch job of supervision thereafter, presumably he would never have a serious "personnel problem." At least, many supervisors seem to believe this. They will tell you that they have "inherited" the people in their unit, along with various problems, and they imply that this is scarcely their fault. Sometimes supervisors are inclined to shrug their shoulders over these inherited problems. "Let personnel take care of it," they say. "This is none of my doing."

Of course, nearly all supervisors do inherit their people, just as the people of a unit often inherit their supervisor. Indifference to the human problems that come along with the people denotes a supervisor unwilling to face realities or unable to solve problems any supervisor must expect to have to deal with sooner or later. Nor is starting with a clean slate a guarantee that problems will not arise. Personnel problems can sprout and grow anywhere, any time. They are usually much harder to solve if they are permitted to go on for a long time. It is far better if they can be nipped in the bud in their early stages.

The curious thing is that the beginnings of a problem case can easily go unrecognized, often for quite a while. Such cases seem characteristically to assume unexpected size before some supervisors recognize them for what they are. The sooner these developing cases can be distinguished, the simpler their solution may turn out to be. An experienced (and capable) supervisor learns to spot symptoms that may be indicative of a developing problem. He can often "sense" such a development because of his thorough knowledge of his people, the work they do, and the general principles of supervision he uses in his work.

A suggestion to the new supervisor: The symptoms usually

consist of some kind of *change* in the attitude, work habits, or behavior of an individual. For example, a man begins to come late for work, not just once, but often. Two people in the unit stop speaking to each other. A man develops a habit of staring out the window. A worker, formerly doing good work, begins turning out sloppy work. These symptoms and many others like them are small matters, but they may indicate something is wrong.

There are two courses of action a good supervisor should not take when he is confronted with a problem case. He should not try to solve it by transferring his case out of his unit. Transfer of a problem child, except as a bona fide move toward better placement, is the mark of inexperience or ineptitude. Unfortunately, there are plenty of supervisors who try this first, without ever seeking to solve the problem where it has arisen. This practice should be condemned wherever it occurs. It denotes a shirking of a primary responsibility that is inherent in the job of every supervisor.

The second course a supervisor should not take is to dump his case in the lap of personnel staff people the moment he recognizes the problem. It is a familiar and plaintive cry of the inept supervisor that "Personnel" or Civil Service ought to *do* something. The staff people of a personnel office cannot be responsible for all the problem cases that arise. They are there to provide expert advice and counsel to supervisors, but the responsibility for dealing with the problem is first of all in the supervisor himself.

Some Suggested Approaches

Certain general rules need to be kept in mind when we approach a problem case, big or little. These rules, or ideas, can help a supervisor to avoid many mistakes, although they cannot be used as a guarantee of success. Some of these ideas have already been noted in Chapter 4, but here we will expand and illustrate their use.

1. Possibly the first question to be answered is whether the supervision itself has been adequate. A conscientious supervisor owes it to himself and his people to ask himself just such a question when a problem arises that may cast doubt on the quality of the supervisory job he has done so far. A useful check list to consider would include the seven principles of supervision discussed in Chapter 2, like this:

a. Does the man really understand clearly what is expected of him? *How do we know this?*

b. Has he really been given appropriate guidance in doing his work? *Sure about this?*

c. Has his good work been recognized? *All of it? When?*

d. Has he been given constructive help in improving his poor work? *When? What happened?*

e. Has he ever been given a real opportunity to show that he can do more responsible work than his position calls for? *How did he do?*

f. In what specific way has he been encouraged to improve himself? *What did he do?*

g. Are his working conditions really satisfactory? *Which ones are? Which ones are not?*

If a supervisor cannot give positive answers to these questions, after careful and thoughtful consideration, then it is possible that the correction of any omissions may help solve the case. First of all, that is, the use of supervisory principles must be correct and complete. Incidentally, a supervisor may find it useful to review this question with his own supervisor, as impartially as he is able. Sometimes he may learn that he does not see the application of supervisory methods in the same way his supervisor does. He should make no attempt here to alibi his work, but rather to enlist help in evaluating his efforts up to date.

2. A second question of great importance is whether the problem case, that is, the human being concerned, is well and fully known. Specifically, a supervisor needs to review such questions as these:

a. What about the man's past history with the organization? What are the facts about his employment, transfers, promotions, performance, and qualifications for his present job?

b. Are there any pertinent facts about the man's home life? Is he in any trouble financially? With his family? From the standpoint of health? In any other way? How do we know this?

c. What facts do we have about his interest in the work he is doing, his attitudes, and his ambitions?

Our point here is to be sure that a man's background and experience are generally pretty well known. Recognizing that we cannot possibly know everything about it, we should still be clear about the salient facts. Unless this is so, trying to solve a problem involving the man may be more difficult or impossible.

3. Next we come to the question that is frequently the most important one of all, namely, "Why?" Why has the man done or failed to do the things in question? Why is his attitude negative? Why does he seem to lack ambition? Why is his work poor? Why has he failed?

Over and over again, an answer to the question "Why?" may give a clue to successful action. If we are not sure of the reasons underlying employee behavior, our efforts to improve it are not likely to be particularly successful. Unless we undertake to find out why the employee has done what he has, or failed to do what we wanted him to, we may find ourselves condemning the man unjustly. We may, in fact, start to take action that has little to do with the real problem. In 1949 Bruce Stewart, writing in *Science*,[1] pointed out:

We have not yet realized the full significance of the elementary principle that there are causes for social phenomena. If we applied that principle, we would renounce such attitudes as blame or condemnation of sin. These attitudes lead us away from an

1. *Science*, 110: 182, 1949.

attack on causes, and therefore away from cure and prevention of human ills. No physicist would kick his apparatus because it didn't work right.

4. As a sort of corollary, it is of great importance that the supervisor *talk* with his problem child. Many cases can be resolved if the supervisor can only encourage his man to talk. This means, as we have noted in Chapter 9, that the supervisor must be skilled in the art of listening.

Frequently the only source of the answer to our "Why?" question is the problem case, that is, the human being himself. He may not always know why he is acting as he does, but sometimes he knows very well. Being human, he may offer many reasons tending to vindicate his attitude or excuse his failure, but if he can be led to talk it out, in the end both he and the supervisor may come to understand the reasons underlying the undesired behavior.

Too many supervisors seem fearful of talking freely with their problem children. They seem to consider it an uncomfortable or distasteful thing to do. But it is not. Not, that is, if the supervisor is seeking to understand. Then it becomes a very interesting and worthwhile thing to do.

We can summarize a number of these points in simple chart form, setting forth useful do's and don'ts. These are based on the experience of a great many successful supervisors:

Do:	Don't:
1. Check your own supervision	1. Ignore small problems
2. Check your knowledge of the man	2. Try to dump the case in the lap of "Personnel"
3. Ask *why*	3. Try to transfer the case just to get rid of it
4. Talk with the man about the problem	4. Treat symptoms; rather, search for the cause

Before we look at a few interesting cases, let us note that our discussion so far has placed a great deal of responsibility on the supervisor. We suggest that people who hope to become proficient in supervision may welcome this responsibility. We suggest also that those who seek to avoid it are well advised to go into some other kind of work.

The cases we discuss below are all described from real life. We have selected them as illustrative of a few of the more common problems, problems that are most likely to confront supervisors. However, no case you may have will prove to be exactly like these, and chances are good you may have a case quite unlike any of them. Furthermore, for reasons of space and to bring out points as sharply as possible, all the full surrounding factors in each case have generally been omitted. We concentrate primarily on facts and factors that had most to do with the problem and its solution.

The Case of the Tardy File Clerk

This problem began in a very simple way, as such cases often do. The vivacious, attractive girl of twenty-five, who worked as a clerk in the filing section of a huge government office, began coming late to work. This was somewhat distressing to all concerned, because the girl was so well liked. Eventually the supervisor called her in, told her this sort of thing could not be tolerated, and warned her to be on time thereafter. For a few days, the file clerk got to work on time. Then she began coming late again.

Over a period of time, despite repeated warnings, she was late to work, and in addition she took too much time for coffee breaks and lunch. The supervisor began to charge her with leave for these periods, and spoke to the girl very strongly about the matter, many times. The supervisor even went over bus schedules with the girl to show her how to get to work at starting time. None of this helped. Finally, the supervisor began to think of discharging her, since her actions were having a decidedly adverse effect on the rest of the people in the unit.

At this point the supervisor sought advice. What should be done? "Everything" had been tried; nothing had worked. Was it not obvious that the girl would have to be discharged? Open-and-shut case, it looked like. But was it?

Careful review and checking on the facts revealed the following points:

1. Our personable file clerk had a college degree in languages. The supervisor did not know this; the personnel file had not been checked.

2. She was fully adept in the use of several foreign languages. This was in the file, too, but the supervisor did not know it. He could have found out by reference to the file or by talking to the girl, or both.

3. The girl took the clerical job because she could not find anything else. She became bored with it, and demonstrated as clearly as possible that she really was not interested in the work she was doing. This, too, the supervisor did not know or realize.

4. All this came to light when the supervisor, *for the first time,* actually sat down and *listened* to what the girl had to say. Before this the supervisor had done all the talking—aimed at getting her to work on time, nothing else.

The upshot of the case was that the supervisor sought the help of staff personnel people. They arranged the girl's transfer to a department where foreign language facility was in demand. Placed in work she enjoyed and was trained for, the "file clerk" did a good job.

In this case the supervisor was unable to solve the case primarily because he made no effort to do anything other than to cure the symptom, lateness to work. He neglected to learn all he could about this particular one of his people. He assumed too much without checking even those facts readily available. And possibly worst of all, he never had a full discussion with his file clerk about her work, her background, her ambitions, her lack of interest in filing—that is, he forgot to ask "Why?"

You may consider this an unusual case, with a too-dramatic ending. And perhaps it is. But let us hasten to note that every case is unusual, even if the solution may not prove as dramatic as in this one. You may consider, too, that the supervisor in this case must have been quite inexperienced, and this is correct. The supervisor had had only a couple of years' experience and no training whatever for the job he was doing. With due regard for these facts, however, let us note that observed defects in a person's work are symptoms; that we must seek to find the underlying reasons for undesirable behavior; and that every case has depth to it, often extending far below the observed symptoms.

In this case we see also that a good job of placement may be of great help. Note, however, that placement was not used to get rid of a tardy file clerk, but to get a qualified language specialist into a suitable position. Actually the problem was well on the way to solution before placement was considered.

The Case of the Distracted Field Man

This problem has to do with a young man of thirty-eight, who worked in an office in a small town, and who had been working for the same organization for some fifteen years. He had a wife and several children, an excellent record in his work, and was well liked by his associates. Then, without apparent reason, his work began to deteriorate. He forgot things he should have remembered to do, failed to meet his goals, generally went down hill. His supervisor noted this early in the game, and made every attempt he could think of to find out why. His record—carefully reviewed—was impeccable. In the meantime, the man became irritable and difficult to talk to. He became curt and abrupt with the public with whom he had to deal every day. After a number of progressively worse months, the supervisor decided in some desperation to recommend his discharge. The record was clear; the man was simply not performing up to reasonable standards, despite his previous fine work; he showed no improvement after repeated attempts to talk with him and help him. The supervisor felt he could not put up with the situation any longer, since, after all, there was a job to be done. So the supervisor took the whole story to his boss, and they talked it all over.

The two supervisors found, after careful and lengthy review, that there was simply nothing that could account for the failure of the man. And undoubtedly this was their most significant finding. People do not do things for no reason at all; behind every facet of a human being's behavior there is a cause, if it can only be found. This was the way the two supervisors reasoned. Then they took action—not to discharge the man, not to penalize him, but to get at the reason behind the failure. The man himself, as a source of information, was by this time unsatisfactory. He had become somewhat sullen and definitely uncommunicative. So the supervisors quietly went to other sources—to the man's associates, to his friends, and finally to his wife. They explained their sincere desire to help the man, that they were trying to discover how they might help him, that they were sure he needed help, but that they were baffled by his unwillingness to cooperate with them. They knew this was uncertain ground; the news was almost sure to get back to the man that they were "checking on him." But they felt their man's record was far too good to be thrown away as wasted.

To make a long story short, they uncovered the fact that the man had made a bad investment financially and was too proud to admit it. His purchase had been unwise; his family security was jeopardized; his preoccupation with the problem had distracted the attention he had formerly given to his job. The effect on the man has already been described. Armed with this information, the two supervisors met with the man and explained sympathetically that they knew about his trouble and wanted to help. The man blustered, denied it, then threw up his hands and admitted the whole thing with considerable emotion. In later consultation the banker holding a mortgage on the property proved willing to cooperate. The property was finally disposed of with very little loss to our distracted employee, and his work righted itself in due course.

In this case we note the need for persistence in getting an answer to "Why?" that makes sense. We also note that supervisors may, on occasion, have to go to considerable lengths to be sure of their facts. How far to go, of course, depends on the situation. Here, an excellent fifteen-year record obviously justified more than ordinary supervisory effort.

The Case of the New Concept

Our next case can best be told in three brief episodes that took place over a period of half-a-dozen months. The story unfolded in a supervisory training course in which a group of supervisors were studying and discussing much of the material in this book. Early in the course the men were reviewing the various factors important in creating job satisfaction or dissatisfaction. The discussion stemmed from the results of the Pittsburgh study described in Chapter 6. One of the supervisors was a newly appointed foreman of a large group of men in an electrical products manufacturing plant. He was voicing his opinion:

"All this stuff may be okay, but I still say it's money that means the most to people. What can you do without money? That's what pays the bills. That's what people go to work for in the first place." He extended his hand and rubbed forefinger against thumb in the ancient gesture. "I say it's cash makes the world go round, and that first and foremost it's pay that motivates people to work."

The second incident developed two months later. In the meantime, each supervisor had been asked to bring in a problem for discussion. This time it was the turn of our electrical products foreman. His problem had to do with getting production in his unit.

"I'm fairly new on my job," he was saying, "but I'm expected to show results. And so far, I'm just not getting them. My men don't seem to be interested in trying to turn out more work, and they couldn't care less whether we're doing better or worse this month than we did last month." What could he do to get his men to work with him?

The other supervisors in the group started probing. Had he put the production problem up to the men? Had he tried to get their participation in solving it? What had he done to gain his men's confidence? Had he shown them in any way that he had confidence in *them?*

No, it turned out, he had done none of these things. His idea was still clear, that well-paid people could be expected to be high-producing—as a matter of course. "And don't think my men aren't paid well," he went on. "They get as high pay as you can get in the business, and there's plenty of bonuses and fringe benefits besides. It just doesn't make sense the way they're not trying."

The discussion went on. How was the quality of the work? If the quantity was low, was the quality, too? On this point, the young foreman was emphatic that at least some of the work being done was first class. He described an exceptionally good design that one of his men had produced only recently.

One of the supervisors in the group asked if the fine job had been recognized in any way. "Well," the foreman said, "I told him he was putting out the kind of work we expected around here." But was the job good enough to write to him about it? Why not put it in writing and get it in the man's record?

Two months later, in the ending sessions of the course, the third part of the story unfolded. When our foreman asked permission to "say a few words," he had difficulty getting started, but he developed enthusiasm as he went along.

"Look," he started, "you guys were telling me a while back about writing letters to men in my outfit who did a good job. I didn't think the idea was very good, but I finally figured what could I lose, so I wrote a couple. I sent one to the fellow I was telling you about—the one who turned out a design that was probably one of the best my outfit ever came up with. And I wrote another one to an old-timer we had, telling him I appreciated his advice about a tough circuit problem we had, and that when we took his advice, things worked out pretty good. Like you guys suggested, I sent a copy of both letters to my boss, who's in charge of our division, and to the personnel office.

"And you know what?" the young foreman exclaimed, "It worked! My boss called me in later on and told me I was doing all right. But the best thing is that my men are working better. It isn't just the production sheets we get either; you can feel it around the office. And besides this," he went on, "I've got the old-timer on my side now, and we're working on the idea of having the men meet once a month to go over how we're doing and how we can do better."

There was more. But there are several points to note. One is that the company itself obviously was encouraging enlightened supervision—both because the foreman was being sent to the supervisory course, and because the foreman's boss commended his action. Another is that when the old concepts—like "money makes the world go round"—do not work, what, indeed, is there to lose by trying newer concepts based on scientific study? Actually the foreman took a step in the new direction that is probably easier to take than almost any other—he began by expressing his appreciation of good work, by according recognition where it was deserved. We do not know about the many factors operating in the foreman's group of people, of course, but we may note that sincere praise is something that can break down many barriers.

Illustrated here is the simple fact, long known from many studies, that a supervisor operating on the basis of unfounded opinion about what people want from their jobs is likely to experience trouble. Once he proceeds on a corrected basis, and does so sincerely, he is likely to begin experiencing a new and different kind of response from his people.

The Case of the Young Man in Trouble

Here we have a young man of twenty-seven who has a wife and a little boy. He had been five years with a government agency, had a satisfactory record, was doing good work. Then, one day, his supervisor got a phone call from a local department store. The young man owed quite a bill, and had not paid anything on it despite repeated letters. Could the supervisor do anything about this?

The supervisor agreed to talk to his man and see if he could get things straightened out. This he did. Our young man was embarrassed. He explained that he had bought a new house recently and was a little hard put financially to take care of everything when it was due, but that he would try to take care of the bill at once.

A few weeks later another creditor called. Payments were overdue. Could the government do anything? More discussion with the young man brought on more embarrassment and another promise to take care of the payments.

Over a period of several months, a number of calls came in, all from creditors, asking that the man pay his long-overdue bills. The latest discussion between the supervisor and his young man brought out that (1) he had contracted to pay more for his house than he could really afford, (2) he and his wife together owed local merchants much more than they could pay, and (3) he and his wife had separated in the meantime. All told, our young man was in considerable difficulty.

Government supervisors with a case like this on their hands face a perplexing dilemma. The man frequently has a good record, does good work, and is officially a desirable man to keep. However, his personal affairs are obviously not well handled, and worse, they become embarrassing to the agency. How should the supervisor proceed?

This question cannot be answered quickly and easily for several reasons. First, the government will not garnishee wages or salaries in order to pay creditors. Second, the "official" government policy with respect to employees in financial difficulties varies with the agency. In agencies where security is of great importance, nonpayment of legitimate debts may be cause for instant dismissal—a bad security risk. In other agencies, a more lenient attitude is taken; employees are given every reasonable opportunity to get their financial affairs arranged, so that they do not interfere with official business. If this cannot be done, the man is ultimately asked to resign. Failing this, the man is discharged.

In this specific case, the young man's supervisor was able to talk over the entire problem with him. It turned out that the total amount of money owed was a large sum, more than the young man could borrow. It also came out that the separation of the employee and his wife was in the hands of lawyers, and that disposing of the home was out of the question until settlement could be effected. It became clear ultimately that the young man's judgment had not been good, and that he had placed himself in jeopardy through a series of quite unwise and even irresponsible decisions. In the end, he was asked to resign and did so, rather than have his record show dismissal.

Let us note that this action was taken by the supervisor with great reluctance. He was aware that the young man needed help—even as he was being asked to resign. The loss of his job put the young man in even worse trouble. This was a hard decision for the supervisor to make, and for the personnel staff people who were called in to give expert advice. The government, however, cannot tolerate actions by its employees that tend to discredit or embarrass the agency. The young man really had no one to blame but himself. He had an indulgent supervisor who tried personally to assist him in every possible way open to him. He chose personally to pursue a cause that led eventually to his own disaster.

The Case of the Religious Candidate

Here we have a government office that was required by the nature of its work to operate every Saturday in addition to the regular five days during the week. Each weekend, in rotation, one of the three supervisors of the unit was expected to be on duty. At the time of this particular case, one of the supervisory jobs was vacant, and there were two candidates for the job.

The first candidate on the promotion list was somewhat better qualified than the second, although both were very good men. The job was accordingly offered to the first candidate, who was quite willing to take it. He stipulated, however, that he would not work on Saturday because his religion prevented him from doing so. After full discussion of the situation with him, it became clear that (1) there was no other way the work could be arranged except to perform part of it on Saturday, and (2) because of this, the first candidate could not undertake the job. The job was therefore offered to the second candidate, who accepted it and was entirely willing to undertake the necessary Saturday work.

Our first candidate thereupon claimed unfair treatment on the grounds that (1) he was the best-qualified man on the promotion list and (2) he was being discriminated against because of his religion. He threatened to appeal the case to the Civil Service Commission, and because of the religious factor, the supervisor of the unit became fearful of possible consequences.

Now it is true that religious discrimination may not be tolerated in the government service. In this case, however, there was clearly no such discrimination, since the protesting candidate had been offered the position ahead of his nearest competitor and had, indeed, been urged to take it. The candidate had refused the job because his religion did not permit him to work on Saturday. Clearly, it was the candidate who had disqualified himself. There was no discrimination on the part of his agency.

The Case of the Supervisor Who Got What He Deserved

A group of twelve people who were stationed in a small city were working on an activity that required at least two employees to be on duty all the time. They had a schedule that provided for a rotation of employees among day, evening, and night shifts. The supervisor had arranged this schedule so that he worked only during the daytime and only Monday through Friday. His people did the rotating.

Official policy of the agency required all employees to meet certain academic requirements in order to advance above a certain level. Furthermore, the agency, encouraged its employees to take college courses that would help qualify them for a promotion. Fortunately, in the city where our unit was, a college offered day and evening classes in exactly the right subjects.

Our problem case developed when two of the employees asked for permission to take one of the college courses. It seemed that the college required regular attendance in the classes. Because of the schedule of rotation among shifts, they could not meet attendance requirements. They were quite willing to be assigned either to day, evening, or night shifts during the school year, if they did not have to rotate from one shift to another. Could this be arranged?

Our unit supervisor commended the employees on their ambition, but was dubious about the effect of assigning them to regular shifts. He must be fair to all his employees, he said, and to be sure everyone was satisfied, he would put the matter to a vote. This he did.

The vote count showed five employees in favor of the idea and six against it. Hence the two employees had to keep on rotating among shifts and, of course, were unable to go to school. The majority, it seemed, was opposed to any further education.

The two employees promptly requested transfers elsewhere, and shortly thereafter got them. People to replace them were hard to find, and several months passed before they were finally recruited and their training begun. In the meantime, the entire staff had to carry additional work, take the more difficult shifts until the new men were trained, and work various unscheduled shifts. Things even got so bad that the supervisor himself had to work many nights and on some of the weekends!

We may consider that what happened to the supervisor and his "majority" served them right. But of course, the minority had to do extra work also, and the effect in total on the people of the unit and on the work itself was bad. Here we have a supervisor who failed to exert leadership. What he should have done was ask his people, "How can we arrange this?" The agency policy was already clear—employees were to be encouraged to take college courses. The schedule could have been rearranged to permit the two men to attend college; and the rearrangement would in itself have been evidence to the rest of the employees that they, too, could go to school if they wanted to go badly enough.

The Case of the End Run

The head of a section with a dozen people in it was promoted to the position of director of the division. Everyone in his old unit liked him and had confidence in him. They hated to see him go, but they were all pleased at his advancement. They got a new supervisor, one of themselves.

The division director was now supervising half-a-dozen section heads, including the new supervisor of his old unit. He was a very busy man, but never too busy to forget his "old bunch." From time to time, one of them dropped in, to his delight, talked over how things were going, brought up a problem or two, chatted awhile.

In the meantime, the new section head of the director's old unit was working at keeping things rolling as well as his former boss did. He was new, and he lacked experience, but he tried hard to gain the confidence of his people. After a time, he noticed that some of his men seemed to know more than he did about what was going on. They were often ready with answers about what to do—they got them from the old boss, now division director. Gradually, our new section head realized that the division director really had not quite given up supervising his old unit. Men in the section were making end runs directly to the old boss, and he was going along with this kind of operation. Knowing that some of his men were very good friends with the old boss, the new section head felt frustrated about what to do. If he tried to stop them, they would go to the old boss who was now his supervisor. If he let them go on short-cutting him, he would never gain control of his unit.

In the real-life case, the new section head put up with the end runs, hoping that eventually they would end. But they did not, and our section head became more frustrated than ever, then bitter. After a good many months, he was sullen and suspicious of his men and of his supervisor, the old boss; he was ready to quit.

What the new section head should have done was to lay the whole matter before his supervisor just as soon as he realized what was going on. He should have explained why the end runs were defeating him, and how this would, in the end, cause difficulty in the whole division. As it happened, the division director would have been glad to cooperate, if he had only realized. By and large, most supervisors of any experience would. The solution to the problem required that cooperation.

If there is any moral here, it is that the longer a problem is let go, the worse it may get. Any supervisor, new or experienced, needs to face up to his problems just as soon as he is sure of his ground. Then he needs to take the best action he can. If the action calls for considerable diplomacy, as this one seemed to, then he should take that kind of action. But whatever he does, he should never let the problem fester and get worse.

The Case of the Up-and-Down Windows

Simple as this case may be, it happens over and over again in countless offices. The usual situation is that there are six to twelve people in a room. Of these, one or two are very sensitive to drafts and want the office warm; one or two others like it cool and prefer plenty of fresh air. The rest of the people usually do not care one way or another. When this situation includes both men and women of various ages and habits, trouble often starts.

One of the men, for instance, begins by opening a window. In a few minutes one of the women marches over and shuts it. Later the man opens it again. And again the woman shuts it. This process seems only amusing at first. Later it gets to be a nuisance. As time goes on, the people may form themselves into two groups—the Ups and the Downs. In certain long-continued situations, the work is seriously interrupted, and the people get angry with each other.

Supervisors need to see that these silly-simple cases do not develop, or if they have already developed and are running out of control, that they are stopped. There are various ways to do this, depending on the people, but possibly the best way is to get the whole group together and put the problem up to them. Try for agreement, but get compromises if agreement is not forthcoming. Then try what the whole group suggests. Frequently this works, but if it does not, then here is one way that usually does:

1. Put the people who dislike the open windows as far away from the windows as possible.

2. Put the open-air boys right next to the windows.

3. Get a thermometer and place it in the center of the room. Get an agreement (or a compromise) on the best temperature—say 70°F.

4. Anyone can look at the thermometer, but only the supervisor takes action to open or close the windows.

The Case of the Passed-Over Candidate

This is the familiar situation in which one man out of three is promoted, and the two unsuccessful candidates complain of unfair treatment, prejudice, office politics, or other skulduggery. Depending on circumstances, there are many ways to deal with this situation, but one thing is very clear: *the supervisor must deal with it.*

The unsuccessful candidates are now unhappy about their jobs because of what they consider unsatisfactory personnel policy. This is a "dissatisfier" factor, as noted in Chapter 6. You may not think their attitude is justified, but this is beside the point. The men are dissatisfied.

Now there must have been a reason or reasons why you chose one man ahead of the other two. This could have been because of differences in ability or personality, or because of judgment as to the men's potentiality for development in the new job. The problem is to convince the unsuccessful men on about five points:

1. That you believe all three are good men.

2. That the job called for certain specific qualifications, as well as a certain personality and potential.

3. That the man you chose came closest to these needs.

4. That for each of the trailing candidates you have in mind (or better, on paper) some additional training and development that will help prepare them for the next opportunity.

5. That you need them, and that you need their support for the man promoted, if this is required.

The Case of the Two Poor Supervisors

Joe, one of a number of engineers in an office, comes in one morning to urge his supervisor to consider a change in construction of a satellite part. He suggests using a single copper wire coated with silver instead of a twelve-strand copper wire, to be conducted in a single insulated tube instead of two tubes, as used heretofore. (The suggestion is technically sound.)

He points out that this change will save weight, space, money, and materials. His supervisor is dubious. "We've always done it with two tubes and copper wire," he says, "and we're getting along fine."

At this point the supervisor's boss comes in, overhears part of the discussion, jumps to the conclusion that Joe is resisting a change being recommended by his supervisor. He speaks strongly to Joe, advising him that his attitude is not good, that useful changes *are* desirable, and that Joe must accept new ideas gracefully. Joe's supervisor says nothing; in fact, he seldom supports his people. The supervisor's boss then leaves. Whereupon Joe turns on his supervisor, and tells him what he thinks of his failure to explain what really was happening, and leaves in a huff.

This case is well-packed with errors. Joe himself made a mistake when he turned on his supervisor, even though he had good reason. Joe's supervisor failed to clarify the situation when *his* boss was speaking strongly to the wrong man. The supervisor's boss was also in error when he undertook to correct Joe; this, if necessary, was up to Joe's supervisor. Besides this, the supervisor's boss apparently jumps to conclusions pretty quickly.

In the meantime, after Joe had a chance to cool off, he realized he was in a bad spot. No more promotions for him, since the two supervisors controlled these. If he quit and tried to get another job, wherever he applied, inquiries would be made of his last company. He would not get a good reference, obviously. If he tried to see his supervisor's boss and straighten out the situation, he'd get his supervisor in trouble, and this wouldn't help. Probably he made a mistake in not speaking up when his supervisor failed to do so. But the events took place quickly, and Joe kept thinking surely his supervisor would say something. The company is a relatively new one. It has no suggestion system yet. And there is no union. As Joe thought it over, it became clear that he couldn't just do nothing.

What actually happened was that Joe and his fellow engineers decided they had enough of a supervisor who never supported his people. So, in a body, they went directly to the supervisor's boss and demanded the removal of the supervisor. They would *all* quit unless this change were made. Since engineers were rather hard to get at the time, the supervisor's boss agreed to do as they demanded. And in a short time, he got the supervisor out. Interestingly enough, he did the job awkwardly, and such a rumpus was raised, that the company replaced *him,* also!

You may or may not agree with this solution. It is worthwhile, though, to study the mistakes. It is unnecessary for a situation like this one to develop—providing a supervisor is performing as a good supervisor should.

13   *Books and Journals*

As we noted in the first chapter of this book, if a supervisor hopes to do a really professional job of supervision, he must do a certain amount of reading. He needs to know the best books in the field, and he must be able to evaluate them. Furthermore, he should see the more important professional magazines or journals, both to learn of new ideas and to pick up information about new books recently published.

We start first with some of the books. They are listed in alphabetical order by the author's or editor's name. This list is a "starter set" of books that most supervisors will find of value. Most of them have been referred to elsewhere in this book, and when this is so, the reference is shown in parenthesis.

Useful Books for Supervisors

Roads to Agreement, by Stuart Chase, with Marian Tyler Chase. New York: Harper & Row, 1951. 250 pages.

In this book Stuart Chase put together all the techniques he could find that might help people to reach agreement. He searched many scientific fields as well as experience. He borrows from conciliations of labor disputes, unanimous jury agreements, and Quaker meetings. How can we work together? How can we improve our relations with each other? He tries to answer questions such as these by describing how such things have been done, here and there, by all sorts of people and groups.

If you are not familiar with the clear writing and easy style of this author, you should be (see especially his *Men at Work* and *The Proper Study of Mankind*).

The Practice of Management, by Peter F. Drucker. New York: Harper & Row, 1954. 404 pages.

Most of the articles or books written by Peter Drucker, of New York University, are highly stimulating. This book is one of his best. You may not always agree with what he says, but he will make you think. He takes delight in reducing to a shambles some of the comfortable ideas one gets from textbooks, as well as our unsupported assumptions and beliefs.

Emphasis and examples here are from business and industrial organizations. Worth reading a number of times. Readers should be warned that Drucker's writing is brilliant, but that no one should be misled by Drucker's emphatic statements into believing that everything he says is gospel.

Motivation Through the Work Itself, by Robert N. Ford. New York: American Management Association, 1969.

A full report of the installation and use of Herzberg's motivational concepts at Bell Telephone. The study deals with the use of the "Satisfier" factors, and the work was performed in a scientific way. The results included increased productivity, reduced turnover, fewer absences from work, fewer employee grievances, and the like. A very important piece of work, and one that merits close study by supervisors.

Motivation and Productivity, by Saul Gellerman. New York: American Management Association, 1963. 304 pages.

A well-written summary (up to 1963) of the contributions of psychology and sociology to management.

The Motivation to Work, by Frederick Herzberg, Bernard Mausner, and Barbara Bloch Snyderman. New York: John Wiley & Sons, 1959. 157 pages.

Possibly one of the most important studies in the field of supervision in recent years. A full discussion of this study is found in Chapter 6.

Work and the Nature of Man, by Frederick Herzberg. Cleveland and New York: The World Publishing Company, 1966. 203 pages.

Summarizes the foregoing book and relates the later findings concerning the Motivator-Hygiene theory of motivation. Treated in Chapter 6 of this book.

Human Relations in Management, edited by S. G. Huneryager and I. L. Heckmann. New Rochelle, N.Y.: South-Western Publishing Co., 2nd edition, 1967. 879 pages.

A reference work including fifty-three articles on most phases of management. Of these, thirty were published since 1960. Contains an excellent selected bibliography and index. Opens the way to further reading.

Bureaucracy, by J. M. Juran. New York: Harper & Row, 1944. 138 pages.

This little book has been out of print for a while, but it will probably not be out of date for many years to come. In it an industrial engineer considers how the government could be improved through the application of known management techniques. He suggests that half as many people as were employed when he wrote the book could do the needed work, but that to achieve this would take years. He proposes five basic ideas that might help to bring this about, and some of these are, indeed, gradually permeating the federal government.

Juran understands, as many industrial engineers do not, the reasons underlying government operation. Furthermore, he sees the parallels in industry. He pokes fun at both government and industry, but gently, and with full sympathy for the underlying causes. This book is a delight to read. It leaves its readers at once amused and thoughtful. Get it from your library.

How to Talk with People, by Irving J. Lee. New York: Harper & Row, 1952. 176 pages.

A book of great value for its treatment of the talking-listening process. Some of the ideas in this book can be found in Chapter 9. Contains an excellent discussion of people's behavior in conferences and of ways for people to reach agreement. The first chapter is a ten-page summary of what is in the book, but do not stop with this. Ideas spill out of every page in the book. Note especially the little gem labeled Chapter IX, which deals with the "soft approach" to an argument. Easy reading, but requires close attention and careful study to be sure you have wrung the last drop out of the material. Some statements are so simply put that you can easily miss the brilliant core of truth in them.

It is worth noting that Dr. Lee made six half-hour motion pictures before his death in 1955. In these he discusses simply but brilliantly the factors that lead to misunderstanding when people talk together. The title of one of the pictures is *Why Do People Misunderstand Each Other?*, and it is a good one to start with. The films are distributed by the Net Film Service, Indiana University, Bloomington, Indiana. A note to them will bring a folder describing the six films, and telling where you can rent or buy them.

A New Approach to Industrial Economics, by James F. Lincoln. New York: The Devin-Adair Company, 1961. 166 pages.

A remarkable book about the Lincoln Electric Company of Cleveland. Discussed in Chapter 5.

Making Management Human, by Alfred J. Marrow. New York: McGraw-Hill Book Co., 1957. 241 pages.

An exceptionally well-written and interesting book, full of useful and practical ideas for supervisors. Emphasis, as noted in the title, is on the human aspects of management. Has a good bit on participation, and treats the subject in a most illuminating way. Also contains good discussions on why people work, incentives, and communications. Illustrated and enlivened by a series of amusing cartoons taken from many sources and poking a little fun at various aspects of management.

The Human Organization: Its Management and Value, by Rensis Likert. New York: McGraw-Hill Book Co., 1967. 258 pages.

Contains the results of research in many companies and organizations over a period of more than twenty years. Treated briefly on page 55. A most important set of ideas about participation as well as organization.

The Human Side of Enterprise, by Douglas McGregor. New York: McGraw-Hill Book Co., 1960. 246 pages.

This is a book that is worth a great deal of thoughtful study. The ideas in it are important. They have had a major effect on the field of management. A brief résumé of McGregor's theory X and theory Y and their application to management is given in Chapter 7, beginning on page 83.

Pygmalion in the Classroom, by Robert Rosenthal and Lenore Jacobson. New York: Holt, Rinehart & Winston, 1968. 240 pages.

Some of the material in this book is treated in Chapter 3, but there is a great deal more of considerable interest in the study. Recommended both for supervisors and educators.

It All Depends, by Harvey Sherman. University, Ala.: University of Alabama Press, 1966. 218 pages.

The subtitle is "A Pragmatic Approach to Organization." The book discusses a completely practical approach to organizational problems, including span of control, delegation of authority, and so on. Interesting, easy reading, valuable for both supervisors and managers.

The Failure of Success, by Alfred T. Marrow. New York: American Management Association, 1972. 339 pages. Of special value in its description of participation and its relation to organization operation and changes.

Magazines and Journals

Listing journals of probable value to supervisors is not too easy. All of these that follow will usually contain at least one article of interest in each issue, and most of them will have several. There are, of course, many other useful periodicals that may occasionally have a good article, or that may have several in one issue. Sometimes such occasional articles or numbers may be quite valuable. But to list every periodical that might possibly have good supervisory material at one time or another would make our "starter set" much too long. The ones listed here should prove useful, at least as a beginning:

Harvvard Business Review. Published bimonthly by the Graduate School of Business Administration, Harvard University. About 10–12 articles; lots of advertising; 180 pages. Cover carries the statement "The Magazine of Thoughtful Businessmen." The magazine is aimed generally at business and industrial concerns; however, definitive articles on new developments in the management field usually appear in this publication. Not necessarily easy reading—as advertised by by the magazine itself. Considered by many the "best" of management magazines.

Management Review. Published monthly by the American Management Association, Inc. "The Month's Best in Business Reading." Contains digests from various magazines and newspapers; usually two to three special features plus a dozen digests; short summaries of other timely articles; a book review section. About 80 pages, digest size.

Training and Development Journal. Official magazine of the American Society for Training and Development. (Formerly the *Training Directors Journal.*) Monthly, about 70–80 pages, 10–15 articles, 12–15 training research abstracts, classified ads, book reviews.

Personnel Journal. "The Magazine of Industrial Relations and Personnel Management." Published by the Personnel Journal, Inc., Swarthmore, Penna. Monthly (July–August issues combined). About 60 pages, 8–10 articles, book reviews, help and positions wanted advertisements, and special features.

Personnel. Published bimonthly by the American Management Association. About 80 pages, 8–10 articles, book reviews, special features.

Personnel Administration. Journal of the Society for Personnel Administration. Contains 6–8 original articles, book reviews, and several special features. Bimonthly. About 60 pages.

Supervisory Management. Published monthly by the American Management Association, Inc. Contains about 12–14 features and digests of articles from other magazines in about equal numbers; book review section, cases, notices of laws, etc. About 60 pages. Somewhat less sophisticated than *Management Review.*

Supervision. "The Magazine of Industrial Relations and Operating Management." Published by Supervision Publ. Co., Mt. Morris, Ill. Appears monthly. Of value primarily to industrial shop foremen. About 30–35 pages.

Nation's Business. Published monthly by the U.S. Chamber of Commerce. Usually contains 1–3 specific management articles.

Index

achievement
  developing need for, 88–90
  expectations and, 23–32
  job satisfaction and, 63–64,
    66–67, 75–76
administration
  climate of, 148
  job dissatisfaction and, 65, 67,
    78–79
  organization and (see also
    Organization), 133
Administrative Science Quarterly,
  viii n, 26 n
Adult Education in a Free Society
  (ed. Kidd), 20 n
Advanced Management, 142 n
advancement
  job satisfaction and, 63,
    64–65, 67, 76–77
  see also Career(s); Promotion
Agriculture Department, Graduate
  School of, viii
Alcoholics Anonymous, 15–16
American Assembly, Report of,
  79 n
American Management Association,
  6 n, 7 n, 88
American Psychologist, 88 n
anger, 120
apprenticeship, 92–93
Argyris, Chris, 149 n
Art of Readable Writing, The
  (Flesch), 126 n
authoritarianism, 6–7
authority
  delegation of, 6, 35–36,
    142–143
  lines of, 137–139
  participation and, 59
  responsibility and, 140
  symbols, disregarding in
    listening, 117
Autobiography (Franklin), 120
awards, 17

Bakke, E. Wight, 55, 57–58
Bavelas, Alex, 24, 30, 31, 55

behavior
  problems, handling, 38–39,
    170–191
  studies, 82–90
  see also Motivation
Bell Telephone, 81 n, 193
Bellows, Carol and Robert, 130 n
Benevolent-Authoritative system,
  86
Berlew, David E., 26 n, 31
Biology and the Future of Man
  (ed. Handler), 28 n
Blakeley, Robert, 20
bonuses, 17
books
  reading, how-to suggestions,
    127–131
  for supervisors, 3, 192–196
  training, personnel, and
    assigned reading, 108–109
"boss," characteristics of, 6–7
bribery, handling, 40–41
Bureaucracy (Juran), 194
Burns, Robert K., 60–61

career(s)
  advancement and job satisfaction,
    63, 64–65, 67, 76–77
  Civil Service, 78–79
  policy, 11
  rate of training and, 103–104
  responsibilities, increased, 18–20
  self-improvement, 1–4, 114–115
  training for, 100–101
Casals, Pablo, 30
case histories
  distracted field man, 177–179
  end run, 186–188
  new concept, 179–182
  passed-over candidate, 189
  religious candidate, 184–185
  supervisor who got what he
    deserved, 185–186
  tardy file clerk, 175–177
  two poor supervisors, 190–191
  up-and-down windows, 188–189
  young man in trouble, 182–184

cash awards and bonuses, 17
Center for Research in Personality
    (Harvard), 88–89
"Changing Patterns in Human
    Relations" (McGregor), 55 *n*
Chase, Marian Tyler, 113 *n*, 192
Chase, Stuart, 113 *n*, 192
chief, 8, 133
Civil Service, 78–79
    see also specific subjects
classification
    of people, stereotypical, 26–29
    personnel, work-load analysis and,
        151–157
Colorado State University, viii
Columbia University, viii
command, unity of, 139–140
commands, direct, 35
communications, 9, 112–113
    brevity, 126–127
    commendatory, 16–17
    films on, 195
    Fog Index, 122–126, 127
    generalizations about, dangerous,
        113
    information, current, 12
    information, specialty and tech-
        nical, 13–15
    listening, rules about, 116–118
    orders, giving, 35
    organization and, 133, 148
    reading, rapid, 129–130
    reading, rules about, 127–129
    reports by personnel, 44–45
    soft vs. hard approach, 120–121,
        195
    sorting, 128–129
    talking-listening process, 114–116
    talking, rules about, 118–121
    writing-reading process, 121–126
conferences
    staff, 13, 43–44
    training, 105–106, 110–111
Consultive system, 86
coordination, 133, 137
costs
    operating, 9
    training, productivity and, 96–99
counseling
    nondirective, listening and, 117
    training and, 109–110
courses for supervisors, 4

criticism, use of, 37
    anger, avoidance of, 120
    constructive, of poor work, 17–18
    personality improvement, 15–16
    soft vs. hard approach, 120–121,
        195

decision making, 36–37
Defense Department, 146, 147
delegation of authority, 6, 35–36, 142–
    143
"Developing Patterns in Manage-
    ment" (Likert), 7 *n*
developmental training, 100–101
"Dignity of the Individual" (Heaton),
    37 *n*
discrimination, religious, 184–185
dissatisfiers, 62–63, 65, 66–68
    company policy and administration,
        65, 67, 78–79
    occupations covered by study of,
        70–71
    performance effects, 68–69
    salary, 65–66, 67, 79–80
    supervision, interpersonal, 65, 66,
        77
    supervision, technical, 65, 77
    supervisors and control of, 77–81
    working conditions, 65, 66, 67, 80–
        81
"Do You Know How to Listen?"
    (Johnson), 118 *n*
drinking on job, handling cases of,
    40–41
Drucker, Peter F., 193
Durea, 25

education, 20–21
    achievement, expectation and, 23–32
    continuing, of supervisors, 4
    course taking by employee, case
        history of, 185–186
    self-improvement, 21
    see also Training, personnel
Ehrlich, Eugene, 130 *n*
employees, *see* Personnel management;
    specific subjects
encouragement, use of
    achievement and, 75–76
    personality improvement, 15
    recognition of good work, 16–17,
        180–181

Etc., 118 *n*
evaluation of training, 105–106
executive, 8
executives, need for achievement and
success of, 89
expectations, achievement and, 23–32
Exploitive-Authoritative system, 86

"Failure of Success" (Marrow), 87–88,
196
fault-finding, 5
favoritism, 5
*Federal Government Service: Its
Character, Prestige, and Problems*
(Report of American Assembly),
79 *n*
financial difficulties, case history of
employee, 182–184
Flesch, Rudolf, 126
Fog Index, 122–126, 127
Ford, Robert N., 81 *n*, 193
foremen, 8
expectations, productivity and, 25
Franklin, Benjamin, 120
Freud, Sigmund, 117
"Function of Management" (Bakke),
58 *n*

Gardiner, Burleigh, 55
Gellerman, Saul, 90 *n*, 193
government agencies, employment,
see specific subjects
Graicunas, 141
grapevine, 13
grievances, settling, 38
group training, 110–111
guidance
supervisory, 8, 13–16
training, personnel, and, 104, 109–
110
Gunning, Robert, and Fog Index,
122–126, 127

Hall, Douglas T., 26 *n*, 31
handbooks, office, 12–13, 45
"hard" vs. "soft" approach, 120–121,
195
Harvard Business Review, 26 *n*, 81 *n*,
141 *n*, 197
Hayakawa, I. S. I., 113 *n*
health hazards, 22

hearing, 114
see also Listening
Heaton, George, 37 *n*
Heckmann, I. L., 194
Herzberg, Frederick, 62 ff., 70 ff., 81,
82–83, 84, 86, 193–194
How to Talk with People (Lee),
119–120, 194–195
Hugh-Jones, E. M., 58 *n*
Human Animal (LaBarre), 34
*Human Organization: Its Manage-
ment and Value, The* (Likert),
7 *n*, 85 *n*, 196
*Human Relations and Modern
Management* (ed. Hugh-Jones),
58 *n*
Human Relations in Management
(Huneryager), 194
Human Side of Enterprise, The
(McGregor), 74 *n*, 83 *n*, 196
Huneryager, S. G., 194

individuality of employees, 33–35
inefficiency, dealing with, 41–43
information, sources and availability
of
for personnel, 10–15
for supervisors, 192–198, 304
training, personnel, and assigned
reading, 108–109
see also Communications; Books;
Magazines and periodicals,
professional
Institute for Social Research (University of Michigan), 85
*Integrating the Individual and the
Organization* (Argyris), 149 *n*
interest
in employee backgrounds, 33–35
in learning, training and, 101–
102
talking-listening process and, 117
interpersonal supervision, 33–35
case history, 182–184
job dissatisfaction and, 65, 66, 77
IQ, expectation and, 24–26
It All Depends (Sherman), x *n*, 137 *n*,
196

Jacobson, Lenore, 23 *n*, 24–26, 27, 31,
196

Job Attitudes: Review of Research and Opinion (Herzberg et al.), 62 *n*
jobs
    dissatisfying factors, 65–66, 72–77
    procedures, improving, 162–169
    satisfying factors, 63–65, 77–81, 179–182
    training for, 12, 95–99
    work-load analysis and, 151–157
    see also Work; specific subjects
Johnson, Wendell, 117–118
journals, professional, 3, 197–198
    see also magazines and periodicals, professional
Juran, J. M., 194

Kellogg, Edward C., 6 *n*
Kidd, J. R., 20 *n*
Korzybski, Alfred, 113 *n*

La Barre, Weston, 34
Language in Thought and Action (Hayakawa), 113 *n*
Leadership and Organization (Tannenbaum, Wechsler and Massarik), vii *n*
leadership, democratic, 7
Leadership on the Job—Guides to Good Supervision (ed. American Management Association staff), 6 *n*
Learch, Archer L., 146
Lee, Irving J., 119–120, 194–195
Leighton, Alexander, 55
Lewin, Kurt, 55
Likert, Rensis, 7 *n*, 55, 58, 85–87, 90, 196
Lincoln Electric Company, 51–54
Lincoln, James F., 51–52, 54, 195
Lincoln, John, 51
listening, 112–116
    authority symbols, disregarding, 117–118
    counseling, nondirective, 117
    hearing the speaker out, 117
    hearing vs., 114
    interest, apparent, 117
    relaxed, 116
    rules about, 116–118
Livingston, J. Sterling, 26 *n*, 31

long-distance supervision, 43–45
loyalty, 5
    failure, case history of, 190–191

magazines and periodicals, professional
    reading, how-to suggestions, 127–131
    for supervisors, 197–198
    training, personnel, and assigned reading, 108–109
maintenance training, 99–100
Making Management Human (Marrow), 195
management
    activities, 150–169
    definition of, 150
    see also specific subjects
"Management and Human Relations" (Urwick), viii *n*
"Management of Learning, The" (Bellows and Bellows), 130 *n*
Management Record, 55 *n*
Management Review, 197
manager, 7–8
"Manager's Span of Control" (Urwick), 141 *n*
"Managing Motivated Employees" (Penzer), 26 *n*
manuals, office, 12–13, 45
Marrow, Alfred, 87–88, 195, 196
Maslow, A. H., 82–83, 84, 86, 90
Massarik, F., viii *n*
Mausner, Bernard, 62 *n*, 193
McClelland, David, 88–90
McGregor, Douglas, 54–55, 60, 74 *n*, 83–85, 86, 90, 196
Meaning of Culture (Powys), 59
meetings, staff, 13, 43–44
memos, 126–127
    see also Communications
Men at Work (Chase), 192
Merton, Robert, 55
misconduct, dealing with, 40–41
mistakes, admission of, 5
motion pictures on communication, 195
motivation, 62–63, 66–72
    case history, 179–182
    developing need to achieve, 88–90
    egoistic needs, 82–83
    job-dissatisfying factors (satisfiers), 65–66, 72–77

motivation (*cont'd*)
  job-satisfying factors (dissatisfiers), 63–65, 77–81
  motivator-hygiene theory, 70–71
  responsibility of supervisor, 8
  system 4 and, 85–87, 90
  theory X and theory Y, 83–85, 86, 90, 196
  training and, 101–102
Motivation and Personality (Maslow), 82 *n*
Motivation and Productivity (Gellerman), 90 *n*, 193
Motivation Through the Work Itself (Ford), 81 *n*, 193
Motivation to Work, The (Herzberg, Mausner and Snyderman), 62 ff., 193
Motivator-Hygiene theory, 70–71
Myers, M. Scott, 81 *n*

National Safety Council, 22
Nation's Business, 198
Navy experiments on talking-listening process, 116–117, 118–119
Net Film Service, 195
New Approach to Industrial Economics, A (Lincoln), 54 *n*, 195
New Patterns of Management (Likert), 85
Nielander, William A., 6 *n*, 37 *n*
North Carolina State University, viii
"Notes on a General Theory of Administration" (Urwick), viii *n*
Nurtured by Love: A New Approach to Education (Suzuki), 29 *n*

office
  environment, 21–22
  rules, 11, 12
orders, giving, 35
organization, 8, 132–133
  authority, lines of, 137–139
  changes in, 145
  climate, administrative, 148
  communications (*see also* Communications), 133, 148
  coordination, 133, 137
  efficiency, 137
  familiarity with, of supervisor, 146–148
  flexibility, 145
  function assignment, 143
  human relations and, 149
  line staff, 133–137
  objectives, 132, 148
  orientation training, 10–13, 94–95
  policy and administration, job dissatisfaction and, 54, 67, 75–79
  principles of, 137–145
  reporting hierarchy, 139–40
  responsibility and authority, supervisory, 140
  review, constant, 144–145
  shake-ups, 145
  simplicity, 143–144
  span of control, 140–142
  staff work, 146, 147
  understanding of by personnel, 11, 12
  unity of command, 139–140
orientation, personnel, 10–13, 94–95

paperwork, excessive, 168–169
participation
  problems in, 58–61
  productivity and, 46–58
  responsibility and, 75
Participative system (system 4), 87–88, 90
Penzer, W. N., 26 *n*
performance
  expectations and, 23–32
  good, recognition of, 16–17, 180–181
  motivation and, 66–72
  poor, constructive criticism of, 17–18
  standards and measurement, 12
personalities, employees as, 33–35
personality improvement, personnel, 15–16
Personnel, 198
Personnel Administration, 130 *n*, 198
Personnel Journal, 26 *n*, 198
personnel management
  expectations, supervisory, 23–32
  placement, 18–20, 74, 156–157
  principles of supervision, 10–22
  problem cases, 38–41, 170–191
  responsibilities of supervisor, 8–9
  techniques, 33–45
  work-load analysis, 151–156
  see also specific subjects
placement policies, 18–20, 74, 156–157

planning, 9, 157–159
  participation in, 59
  training, personnel, 93, 105, 106–108
policy, company
  job dissatisfaction and, 65, 67,
    78–79
  job procedures and, 167–169
Powys, John Cowper, 59
Practice of Management, The
  (Drucker), 193
problem cases, handling, 170–175
  end run, 186–188
  field man, distracted, 177–179
  file clerk, tardy, 175–177
  misconduct, 40–41
  new concept, 179–182
  passed-over candidate, 189
  problem child, 38–39, 171
  religious candidate, 184–185
  supervisor who got what he
    deserved, 185–186
  supervisors, two poor, 190–191
  windows, up-and-down, 188–189
  young man in trouble, 182–184
  see also Criticism, use of
*Proceedings Fifth Anniversary Con-
  vocation of the School of
  Industrial Management, Massachusetts Institute of Technology,*
  83 n
productivity
  expectations and, 25
  job training and, 95–99
  participation and, 46–58
promotions, 17, 18–20
  end run vs. cooperation, case
    history, 186–188
  job satisfaction and, 63, 64–65, 67,
    76–77
  passed-over candidate, handling,
    189
  religion as issue, case history, 184–
    185
  see also Career(s)
Proper Study of Mankind (Chase),
  192
publications for supervisors, 3, 192–
  198
  see also magazines and periodicals,
    professional
"*Pygmalion in Management*"
  (Livingston), 26 n

Pygmalion in the Classroom
  (Rosenthal and Jacobson), 23 n,
  24–26, 196

raises, 17
reading
  assigned, and personnel training,
    108–109
  rapid, 129–131
  rules about, 127–129
  sorting, 128–129
  writing process and, 121–124
Readings in Management (Richards
  and Nielander), 6 n, 37 n
recognition, 6
  achievement and, 76
  of good work, 16–17, 180–181
  job satisfaction and, 63, 64, 67, 76
red tape, 162–163, 169
refresher training, 99–100
Reid, T. Roy, vii
religion as issue, 184–185
reports by personnel, 44–45
  brevity, 126–127
  see also Communications
Research Center for Group Dynamics,
  55
responsibility, employee
  increasing, 18–20
  job satisfaction and, 63, 64, 67, 74–
    75
  participation and, 75
Richards, Max D., 6 n, 37 n
Roads to Agreement (Chase and
  Chase), 113 n, 192
Rosenthal, Robert, 23 n, 24–26, 27, 31,
  196

safety, 21–22
salaries
  garnisheeing, 183
  job dissatisfaction and, 65–66, 67,
    79–80
  job training, productivity and,
    96–99
  raises, 17
satisfiers, 62–63, 64–68
  achievement, 63–65, 66–67, 75–76
  advancement, 63, 64–65, 67, 76–77
  occupations covered in studies of,
    70–71
  performance effects, 68–69

satisfiers *(cont'd)*
  recognition, 63, 65, 67, 76
  responsibility, 63, 64, 67, 74–75
  supervisor and control of, 72–77
  work itself, 63, 64, 67, 73–74
Saturday Evening Post, 130 *n*
Scanlon, Joseph, 55
scheduling, 9, 159–161
  training, personnel, 105, 107–108
Science and Sanity (Korzybski), 113 *n*
self-analysis, 4
self-improvement
  personnel, 20–21
  supervisors, 1–4
semantics, 114–115
  see also Communications
shake-ups, 145
Sherman, Harvey, x *n*, 137 *n*, 196
Snyderman, Barbara B., 62 *n*, 193
"Socialization of Managers: Effects of
  Expectations on Performances"
  (Berlew and Hall), 26 *n*
societies, professional, 3
"soft" vs. "hard" approach, 120–121,
  195
span of control, 140–142
"Span of Control—Fact or Fable,
  The" (Suojanen), 142 *n*
"Speed Reading Is the Bunk"
  (Ehrlich), 130 *n*
staff meetings, 13, 43–44
staff organization, 133–149
  see also Organization
Stevenson, Adlai, 31
Stewart, Bruce, 173–174
students, college, 19
Suojanen, W. W., 142 *n*
supervision
  interpersonal, 33–35, 65, 66, 77
  kinds of, 5–7
  long-distance, 43–45
  poor, characteristics of, 5–6
  principles, basic, 10–22
  technical, 14–15, 65, 77
  techniques, 33–45
  see also Supervisors; specific
    subjects
Supervision, 198
supervisors
  authority, 6, 35–36, 140, 142–143
  backgrounds, and designation as,
    1–2

development of, 2–4
expectations of, performance and,
  26–32
information and knowledge sources,
  3–4, 192–198
kinds of, 5–8
management activities, 150–169
motivating employees, 72–81
poor, case history of two, 190–191
problem cases, solving, 170–191
promotion: case history of end run
  vs. cooperation, 186–189
responsibilities, 8–9, 140
span of control, 140–142
see also Supervision; specific
  subjects
Supervisory Management, 198
Survey Research Center, 55
Suzuki, Shinichi, 29–32
system, 4, 85–87, 90

talking, 112–116
  anger, avoidance of, 120
  finality, avoidance of, 119–120
  generalities, avoidance of, 119
  listeners, thinking about, 118
  rate of speaking, 119
  rules about, 118–121
  soft vs. hard approach, 120–121
  "talking down," 120
Tannenbaum, R., viii *n*
tardiness, case history of handling,
  175–177
technical supervision, 14–15, 65, 77
Technique of Clear Writing
  (Gunning), 122–126, 127
techniques
  information concerning, 14–15
  supervisory, 33–45
Texas Instruments, 81 *n*
"That Urge to Achieve" (McClelland),
  88
theory X and theory Y, 83–85, 86, 90,
  196
Think, 88 *n*
"Top-Flight Supervisor: A Profile"
  (Kellogg), 6 *n*
top management, definition of, 150
"Toward a Theory of Motive
  Acquisition" (McClelland), 88 *n*
Training and Development Journal,
  197–198

training, personnel
  apprenticeship, 92–93
  career or developmental, 100–101
  conferences, 105–106, 110–111
  cost and productivity, 96–99
  definition of, 91
  demonstration, 110
  evaluation, 105–106
  group training, 110–111
  guidance and counseling, 104,
    109–110
  interest and, 101–102
  job training, 95–99
  kinds of, 93–94
  maintenance or refresher, 99–100
  methods, 108–111
  orientation, 10–13, 94–95
  performing work, 104
  planning, 105, 106–108
  principles of, 101–106
  rate, 103–104
  reading, assigned, 108–109
  responsibilities of supervisor, 8,
    10–13, 91, 102–103
  scheduling, 105
  self-improvement, 20–21
  "send-him-out-with-Joe" school,
    92–93
  "sink-or-swim" school, 92
  suitability to individual, 102
  systematic, 93
  tests, 106
  trial and error, 92
  visual aids, use of, 111
  written communication, 110
trial-and-error learning, 92
Tyranny of Words (Chase), 113 *n*

United States Navy, 116–117, 118–119
unity of command, 139–140
Uris, Auren, 6 *n*
Urwick, Lyndall F., viii *n*, 141 *n*

visits to plants, and long-distance
    supervision, 44
visual aids
  films on communication, 195
  training, use of, 111

Wechsler, I. R., viii *n*
Western Electric Company, 46–51,
    59
"Who Are Your Motivated Workers?"
    (Myers), 81 *n*
*Why Do People Misunderstand Each
    Other?* (Lee; film), 195
work
  deteriorating, case history of,
    177–179
  good, recognition of, 16–17, 180–
    181
  habits, 162
  improvement studies, 162–169
  job satisfaction and, 63, 64, 67,
    73–74
  job training, 12, 95–99
  loads, analysis of, 9, 151–156
  orientation in job, 11–12
  planning, 9, 157–159
  plans, personnel, 43
  poor, constructive criticism of,
    17–18
  scheduling, 9, 159–161
  specialty information, 13–14
  staff, 146, 147
  standards of quality and quantity,
    12
  techniques, information on, 14–15
  see also Jobs
Work and the Nature of Man
    (Herzberg), 71 *n*, 193–194
Work-improvement studies, 162–167
  need, indicators of, 168–169
  persons to conduct study, 166–167
  steps in, 167–168
working conditions, 11, 12, 21–22
  job dissatisfaction and, 65, 66, 67,
    80–81
  productivity, participation and,
    46–51
  windows, case of the up-and-down,
    188–189
writing-reading process, 121–124
  brevity, 126–127
  Fog Index, 122–126, 127
  reading, rapid, 129–131
  reading, rules about, 127–129

76 77 10 9 8 7 6 5 4 3